The BATTLE of ANTIETAM

The Bloodiest Day

D1416334

Ted Alexander

Charleston   London

THE
History
PRESS

Published by The History Press
Charleston, SC 29403
www.historypress.net

Front cover: Colorized version of a sketch by Edwin Forbes of the 9th New York at Antietam. The black-and-white version appeared in *Frank Leslie's Illustrated Newspaper*, October 11, 1862. *Courtesy of Antietam National Battlefield.*

Back cover: Burnside Bridge. *Courtesy of the Library of Congress.*

First published 2011

Manufactured in the United States

ISBN 978.1.60949.179.6

Library of Congress Cataloging-in-Publication Data

Alexander, Ted.
The Battle of Antietam : the bloodiest day / Ted Alexander.
p. cm.
Includes bibliographical references and index.
ISBN 978-1-60949-179-6
1. Antietam, Battle of, Md., 1862. I. Title.
E474.65.A53 2011
973.7'336--dc23
2011029176

Dedicated to

Joe Harsh, who set the standard for all of us who study Antietam

And to Patrick Roy, who gave his all for his country

Contents

Foreword

September 17, 1862, was unlike any other day during the Civil War—in fact, in American history. A fury descended upon the farmers' fields and woodlots along Antietam Creek outside Sharpsburg, Maryland. By sundown, roughly twenty-three thousand Americans—fellow citizens less than two years before—had been killed, wounded or captured. The bloody harvest remains unparalleled in the nation's past.

The carnage staggered the survivors in both armies. It was beyond their experience and seemingly beyond comprehension. "When I think of the Battle of Antietam it seems so strange who permits it," confided surgeon William Child of the 5th New Hampshire in a letter to his wife on October 7. "To see or feel that a power is in existence that can and will hurl masses of men against each other in deadly conflict—slaying each by thousands—mangling and deforming their fellow men is almost impossible. But it is so—and why we can not know."

It might have been, as Child tried to understand, that an unknown and unseen force had engulfed the landscape around the Maryland village, exacting a terrible price before passing on. More likely, it might have been the belief among the foes—Yankee and Rebel—that the battle's outcome could determine the country's fate. Would the Union be saved, or would the Confederacy achieve independence?

Since the final week of June, the conflict had been redirected in the East. During the winter and spring of 1862, the Federals had fashioned a series of victories at Forts Henry and Donelson and at Shiloh. They had captured Nashville and New Orleans. Major General George B.

McClellan's Army of the Potomac had advanced up the Virginia Peninsula to the outskirts of Richmond. So confident was it of ultimate victory in the Confederate capital, the War Department closed recruiting offices throughout the North.

When Confederate general Joseph E. Johnston fell wounded at the Battle of Seven Pines or Fair Oaks on May 31, President Jefferson Davis appointed General Robert E. Lee to temporarily command the Army of Northern Virginia. As Davis's military advisor, Lee reasoned that the Confederacy could not gain its independence if it acted passively against the numerically and materially superior North. Lee decided that he must act aggressively, a calculated boldness that might overcome the long odds against the South. Audacity came to be a central characteristic of Lee's generalship.

The Confederates advanced against McClellan's army on June 26, initiating the Seven Days' Campaign. By week's end, the Federals had been forced out of their works outside the Confederate capital and retreated down the peninsula to a base protected by Union gunboats on the James River. The campaign's outcome secured Richmond and gave Lee and his army the strategic initiative in the East.

In the following weeks, Lee turned his army north toward another Union command, Major General John Pope's Army of Virginia. Using a broad turning or flank movement, brilliantly executed by Major General Stonewall Jackson's renowned "foot cavalry," Lee forced Pope to abandon the Federals' line along the Rappahannock River and to retreat toward Washington, D.C. The clash between the armies occurred on the old battleground along Bull Run on August 29 and 30. The Confederates swept the Yankees from the field in a stunning victory at Second Manassas.

From the plains of Manassas, the Rebels marched northwest toward the fords of the Potomac. "The present," Lee wrote to Davis on September 2, "seems to be the most propitious time since the commencement of the war for the Confederate Army to enter Maryland." Lee admitted that movement beyond the Potomac entailed risks, but he ordered his army across the river. By nightfall of September 6, the Southerners were encamped in and around Frederick, Maryland.

In Washington, meanwhile, President Abraham Lincoln faced a crisis. Several of his cabinet members blamed McClellan for Pope's defeat at Second Manassas, accusing the commander of the Army of the Potomac of withholding reinforcements from Pope. Lincoln understood, as he put it, that "McClellan has the army with him." The beleaguered president assigned McClellan to command the unified armies. A talented organizer,

"Little Mac," as his men called him, restored order, integrated Pope's units into his army and started north in pursuit of Lee.

Ultimately, Lee's daring and misfortune redirected the campaign. While at Frederick, the Confederate commander decided to divide his units, assigning Jackson and five infantry divisions to the capture of the Union garrison at Harpers Ferry, Virginia. While these troops marched on the town, the rest of Lee's army crossed South Mountain en route to a possible movement into Pennsylvania. The trailing Federals, meanwhile, entered Frederick, where soldiers found in a field a copy of Lee's orders that described the Confederate movements. McClellan reacted to the intelligence by advancing toward the mountain range. A daylong engagement ensued at the gaps of South Mountain on September 14, with the Rebel defenders resisting until nightfall.

Throughout the next two days, the armies converged on Sharpsburg and surrounding countryside. The garrison at Harpers Ferry surrendered to Jackson on the morning of September 15, which allowed Jackson to begin sending some of his divisions back across the Potomac to join the army's main body of troops behind Antietam Creek. The capture of Harpers Ferry convinced Lee to make a stand until the army's scattered units could be reunited. "It was better to have fought in Maryland than to have left it without a struggle," he explained in a postwar interview.

McClellan spent September 16 reconnoitering the enemy's ranks beyond the stream and readying the army for an offensive strike. Late in the afternoon, the Union First Corps forded the creek and moved into position north of the Confederate's left flank. More Federal troops prepared to join in the planned daylight assault. Skirmishing flared at times, a harbinger of the approaching struggle. A fog settled in among the woods, hollows and fields of grain during the night.

Before the mists had lifted on Wednesday, September 17, the Federals charged. A Union lieutenant likened the ensuing combat to "a great tumbling together of all heaven and earth." The killing and maiming etched new names in America's past: Miller's Cornfield, East Woods, West Woods, Dunker Church, Sunken Road and Burnside's Bridge. The Confederates barely hung on to the ground, and only the arrival of Jackson's last division from Harpers Ferry saved Lee's army from a possible crushing defeat. Lee stated later that the fight at Sharpsburg or Antietam was his army's finest hour.

Lee held the battlefield for another day before retreating into Virginia. A rear-guard clash occurred at Shepherdstown on September 20, resulting in a Union rout. But the Federals had won a strategic victory in forcing the Confederates out of Maryland. On September 22, Lincoln issued the preliminary Emancipation Proclamation, giving slaves the hope of freedom if the Union prevailed.

This book, written by Ted Alexander, chief historian at Antietam National Battlefield, offers a fresh and compelling account of the momentous campaign and battle. Alexander's knowledge of the operations in Maryland and of the battlefield itself is unsurpassed and reflected in this work. His familiarity with sources, terrain and human interest stories make it a most welcome modern study.

Although the battle is the central feature of the book, Alexander presents much more beyond the strategy and tactics. New material, none found elsewhere, enhances the story. A reader will find chapters on pre–Civil War Sharpsburg and its environs, on the opposing armies, on the battle's aftermath and its impact on civilians and on creation of the national park. It is a rewarding journey through these pages.

Jeffry D. Wert

Preface and Acknowledgements

Why another book on Antietam? The answer to that question has its roots for me more than fifty-five years ago, when I was in first grade. I was born in Tupelo, Mississippi. My dad, a native of northeast Mississippi, died when I was an infant. My widowed mother moved back to her hometown of Greencastle, Pennsylvania, a few miles north of the Mason-Dixon line. This place is strategically located just thirty-five miles from Gettysburg and twenty-seven miles from Antietam. I had shown an interest in history at a very young age. One weekend, my mother decided to take me to Gettysburg. My grandmother came along. She wanted to see where "Dad" had fought ("Dad" was Corporal William Palmer). Being a native of the mountainous area of Frederick County in western Maryland, he was a Unionist, as mountaineers in many Southern states tended to be. Accordingly, he served in the 1st Maryland Potomac Home Brigade, one of several Union regiments raised in this divided state.

The trip to Gettysburg worked wonders. I came away with a cannon, a toy soldier and two postcards. One of the postcards was of a painting of General Lee, and the other was of General Meade. I excitedly brought these items to school for show and tell. When I explained to one classmate that Meade was a Yankee, he kept joking that the good general must have been a baseball player! No matter, I was forever after hooked on the Civil War.

My interest was further fueled by the stories I heard from my grandmother as she talked with the older neighbor ladies on our patio about her dad and their dads in the war. Then there were the summer trips to Tennessee, Mississippi and Louisiana to visit assorted kinfolk and friends. Granddad Alexander would also talk about "Dad." His father, James Alexander, served in the 31st Mississippi Infantry, joining at age fifteen and serving in the Vicksburg Campaign. These summer stays in the Deep South solidified my interest in my dual heritage and the Civil War. Along the way on these sojourns, we visited places like Lookout Mountain, Shiloh and Vicksburg.

Meanwhile, when we were back in Pennsylvania, my dear mom—dutifully and, yes, sometimes wearily—took me to Gettysburg at least once or twice a month. Then, one weekend when I was about seven or eight years old, she decided a change of pace was in order. We took a trip to Antietam Battlefield. This was a strange sort of place. There weren't all the monuments that were at Gettysburg, and where were all the gift shops? Indeed, at the time, there was only one: the Lohman's souvenir stand on Bloody Lane. At the time, much of this land was still in private hands. There was a small museum in the lodge building, the Antietam National Cemetery and occasionally you would see a park ranger.

My interest in Antietam did not take immediately. My neighbor's Sunday school class took a field trip to Antietam, and Mom and I were invited to go along. The tour guide was my neighbor's cousin, local historian and educator E. Russell Hicks. His presentation, although verbose, brought the battle to life. Meanwhile, Mom would take me to Miss Virginia Carmichael's bookstore in Hagerstown. I was starting to read beyond the standard children's books on history. In 1960, Mom bought me *September Echoes*. Written by local author John Schildt, this study of the Maryland Campaign and the Battle of Antietam was one of the first adult-level books I ever read. Since then, as an adult years later, I have become good friends with John.

Soon, as the Civil War centennial was in full swing, Antietam began to equal, if not replace, my interest in Gettysburg. In September 1962, I attended the reenactment of the Battle of Antietam; this was the last battle reenactment conducted on National Park Service property. It was staged just beyond the new visitors' center that was being built at the time. Little did I realize that one day I would be working in that building.

Fast-forward a few years. In high school, it wasn't cool to like history. Girls and rock and roll were more fun. But I did date a girl from Sharpsburg for a few years. Then came the Vietnam War. I joined the U.S. Marine Corps and served a tour and a half in Vietnam. By the end of my service stint, I was home with a wife and a baby. The peacefulness of domestic life got me interested again in my history books. At a church camp meeting in the summer of 1973, an evangelist suggested that I go to college.

Fast-forward to 1985. I had been with the National Park Service full time and seasonal for almost five years. Through the workings of a very good man, Paul Chiles, retired Antietam ranger/historian, I was transferred to Antietam National Battlefield. In 1992, I became the battlefield historian. A lifetime goal was achieved. I was blessed.

Now, once again, why another book on Antietam? To date, there have been a number of fine works that examine the Maryland Campaign and the Battle of Antietam. These works tell of the military operations and tactics very well. Through this study, I am attempting to use some of the more recent scholarship to explain Antietam as a place in time, beyond the combat. In this book, it is hoped that the reader will come away with a better understanding of the opposing forces, the Sharpsburg community, the horrible aftermath of the battle and the history of the formation of the battlefield park.

To be sure, I am standing on the shoulders of many great Antietam scholars in this endeavor. Some of them are no longer with us, though their works remain. Joe Harsh was a dear friend and one of our greatest Antietam scholars. He revolutionized Antietam studies through the extensive use of the papers of Colonel Ezra Carman, historian of the Antietam Battlefield Board. I had the honor and pleasure to spend many hours with Joe at seminars, on tours and most often discussing all things Antietam over a meal and some drinks. All too soon, he left this world, but his body of work stands as a tribute to this great scholar.

Jay Luvass visited the battlefield hundreds of times with U.S. Army staff rides from the War College at Carlisle. It was great to call him a friend and to listen to his insights into the Civil War and its connection to the larger scope of military history, such as the age of Napoleon and the generalship of Frederick the Great.

Jim Murfin's *Gleam of Bayonets* is still one of our best Antietam books. He was another friend with whom I was able to share many good conversations about the battle.

Many people have played a role in making this book project happen. I could not have finished this book without the help of good friend and premier Antietam guide Steve Recker. He assisted with the images, the index and other computer-related technicalities. He also reviewed many of the chapters and provided insightful comments.

Many thanks also go to Nick Picerno. He is a longtime friend and the world's leading authority on the 10th Maine Infantry. Nick graciously provided access to his personal collection and loaned a number of images and letters that appear in this study.

I greatly appreciate the contributions of old friend and nationally acclaimed author and historian Jeff Wert. I am honored to have him write the introduction and for his review of the manuscript.

A number of friends gave me access to their personal collections of letters and images. They are Brad Frobush, Scott Hann and Joe Stahl.

Tom Clemens of the Save Historic Antietam Foundation has done much in leading the preservation battle for both the Antietam National Battlefield and surrounding sites associated with the Maryland Campaign. He is also the leading authority on Ezra Carman. I owe him much for his review of this book and his comments.

Antietam National Battlefield cultural resources historian and good friend Keven Walker was very helpful in the editing of this manuscript. He also provided many useful observations regarding the farmsteads on the battlefield.

Former Antietam National Battlefield ranger/historian and artillery expert Paul Chiles has provided much information on the guns, other weapons and equipment of the battle.

Many of the staff of Antietam National Battlefield have provided valuable comments and insights for this book. Among them are Brian Barasz, Joe Calzarette, Mannie Gentile, John Hoptak, K.C. Kirkman, Alann Schmidt and Keith Snyder.

I owe a debt of gratitude to retired Antietam National Battlefield superintendent John Howard and Interpretive Division chief Stephanie Gray. Over the years, they have supported my research trips from New York City to New Orleans, where I acquired copies of soldiers' letters, diaries and memoirs for the Antietam National Battlefield Library.

Dear friends Scott and Kathy Anderson assisted me with images and with the transcription of certain texts.

The maps in this book are by Steve Stanley. He is perhaps the leading cartographer of Civil War battle maps in the United States.

Many others have assisted in various ways with this book or over the years with my research. They include Vince Armstrong, Doug Bast, Ed Bearss, Frank Cooling, Kathlenn Ernst, Dennis Frye, John Frye, Lance Herdegen, Jerry Holsworth, John Nelson, Phil Roulette, John Schildt, Tim Snyder, Richard Sommers and Susan Trail.

A big thanks goes out to my editor, Hannah Cassilly, for all of her help and her patience.

Lastly, my thanks go out to my mother, Jane Alexander, for nurturing my interest in the Civil War and for all those trips to Gettysburg and Antietam more than fifty years ago.

1
High Tide

Imagine a river...about 500 yards wide, from two to three feet deep, the water very swift. Now it is just as full of men as it can be for 600 or 700 yards, up and down, yelling and singing all sorts of war and jolly songs, and in this connection you must find room for eight or twelve regimental bands in the river all the time, the drums beating, the horns a tootin and the fifes a screaming, possibly every one of them on a different air, some "Dixie," some "My Maryland, My Maryland," some "the Girl I Left Behind Me," some "Yankee Doodle." All the men are apparently jolly. I, at least did not feel very jolly, though I imagine some of them contemplated the serious side of the situation.

This was the recollection of Private John W. Stevens of the 5th Texas, written sometime after the war. Stevens went on to write, "I could not for the life of me suppress a feeling of sadness as I beheld this vast concourse of humanity wading the river, so full of music and apparently never once thinking that their feet (many of them) would never press the soil on the south side of the Potomac again." Indeed, Stevens, his fellow Texans and many other young Southerners were about to embark on one of the bloodiest campaigns of the Civil War.[1]

The year 1862 was the decisive one of the war. Indeed, many historians consider it the true high tide of the Confederacy. It was the high tide in many ways: Militarily, the South mounted offensives on a one-thousand-mile front in the late summer and fall of 1862. Economically, the South was severely crushed by the loss of the majority of its major ports in 1862.

Diplomatically, it was checkmated by Lincoln's Emancipation Proclamation after Antietam in the late summer of 1862. Morale on the homefront was severely challenged in 1862, with major losses on the battlefield and devastation to thousands of miles of territory and major cities.

The late historian Bell Wiley, in his insightful book *The Road to Appomattox*, presented one of the first attempts to analyze Confederate defeat more than fifty years ago. Esteemed historian James McPherson takes this theme further in his book *Crossroads of Freedom: Antietam, the Battle That Changed the Course of the Civil War*. He goes further than Wiley in that he provides a good and coherent analysis of the diplomatic sphere of operations during that period without being dry and pedantic, as that subject can tend to be.[2]

The Confederacy was on a roll in the summer of 1861. Union forces had been soundly defeated at First Manassas and Wilson's Creek. The Battle of Ball's Bluff, on October 20, 1861, was a minor affair with little strategic importance, yet it would cast a long shadow. It was fought with about 1,700 men on each side. However, the Rebs were veterans, and the Yanks were green. The fight, just upstream from the nation's capital near Leesburg, Virginia, ended in a Union rout. Indeed, it was a massacre as the green Yankees leaped to their deaths in the river or were shot as they tried to swim or board nearby rowboats. More than 200 Union soldiers were killed or wounded and another 714 captured or missing. Confederate losses were 33 killed and 115 wounded or missing.[3]

The nation was shocked—especially the Lincoln family—when one of the Union commanders at Balls Bluff, Colonel Edward Baker, was killed. Baker had been a close friend of the president, dating back to their Illinois legislative years. He had served as a legislator from Illinois, as a volunteer officer in the Mexican War and as senator from Oregon. The Lincoln family so admired him that they named one of their sons Edward Baker Lincoln.

These Confederate victories gave rise to overconfidence in the South. Zealous politicians and editors echoed the belief in Southern superiority. John M. Daniel, in an editorial in the *Richmond Examiner* on September 27, 1861, proclaimed, "The battle of Manassas demonstrated, at once and forever, the superiority of the Southern soldiers, and there is not a man in the army, from the humblest private to the highest officer, who does not feel it. The enemy knows now that when they go forth to the field they will encounter a master race."[4]

But by late 1861 and into early 1862, the tide had begun to turn against the Confederacy. One of the first events in this negative turn involved the largest naval land-sea operation ever launched by U.S. forces until World War II. The Port Royal Expedition of November 1861 would usher in the Union blockade.

With fifty ships (not counting twenty-five coal vessels that had departed the day before) and sixteen thousand soldiers and sailors, Captain Samuel F. DuPont departed Hampton Roads, Virginia, on October 29, 1861. The destination was Port Royal Sound, South Carolina. It was an unpleasant voyage, and heavy gales off Cape Hatteras threatened the success of the expedition.

On November 3, the flotilla managed to reach its destination, but not without some casualties. The USS *Isaac Smith* had to throw its armament overboard to keep from sinking. The *Governor*, a transport ship with a battalion of marines on board, did sink, and some twenty marines drowned.

However, the Confederates were outnumbered, outgunned and outshipped. Two forts guarded Port Royal Sound with about fifty guns, twelve hundred men and three gunboats. DuPont's flotilla literally shelled the Confederates into submission, and Port Royal's defenses surrendered on November 7. This victory was great for morale in the North. And it was the first of many combined army-navy operations during the war.

By the way, in 1860, the U.S. Navy had forty-two warships. By 1861, it possessed eighty-two ships with 7,600 men. By 1865, six hundred naval ships were in operation, and 51,500 men were serving.[5]

This was the beginning of a series of coastal victories by the North. By the spring of 1862, Roanoke Island, New Bern and Fort Macon, North Carolina; Fort Pulaski, Georgia; and Pensacola, Florida, had fallen into Union hands. This meant both loss of ports for commerce and loss of forts.

In March 1862, Confederate forces in Northern Virginia, under Joseph E. Johnston, evacuated their base around Centreville, leaving valuable supplies behind. Meanwhile, Lincoln had found a general with potential. Major General George B. McClellan had won a number of small victories against the Confederates in western Virginia. He was brought back east to take command of a new army dubbed the Army of the Potomac. In April, this army, led by McClellan, began the movement to take Richmond that became known as the Peninsula Campaign.

In May, the Confederates abandoned Norfolk, and the ironclad CSS *Virginia* (aka *Merrimac*), unable to navigate the shallower depths of the James River, was blown up rather than face capture by Union forces. These events had a profound influence on Southern morale. The *New York Times* announced that the fall of Norfolk "was second in importance only to that of New Orleans." The loss of the CSS *Virginia* prompted Confederate ordnance chief Josiah Gorgas to state, "No one event of the war, not even the disaster of Ft. Donelson, created such a profound sensation as the destruction of this noble ship." The James River was now open to within seven miles of Richmond. As McClellan moved on Richmond, panic set in, causing members of the Confederate Congress to rush home and President Jefferson Davis and other cabinet members to send their families farther south.[6]

In the Western Theater, the situation was even more disastrous. The fall of Forts Henry and Donelson in February 1862 was a crippling blow that cost valuable manpower: fifteen thousand prisoners. It also led to the capture of Nashville soon after. This was the first of the Confederate state capitals to fall. A valuable center for horse trading, Nashville also gave the Federals access to key waterways leading to the heart of the South and the collapse of western Tennessee.

The bloody Battle of Shiloh, on April 6–7, 1862, was another Union victory that grasped more territory from the Confederacy. It also cost the life of General Albert Sydney Johnston, who was mortally wounded there. Johnston was one of the first national heroes of the Confederacy and the highest-ranking Confederate general killed in the war. Within weeks, the Confederates abandoned their base at the important rail center of Corinth, Mississippi, leaving it to be occupied by the Union.

On April 8, the Confederate stronghold at Island #10 on the Mississippi River fell to a combined Union army and navy force. This victory yielded approximately seven thousand Confederate prisoners.

On April 25, New Orleans, the largest city in the Confederacy and a key urban center and port, fell to Union admiral David G. Farragutt. On June 6, 1862, the important river town of Memphis was captured by the Yankees.

Meanwhile, in the Trans-Mississippi West, things were no better for the Confederacy. The Union victory at Pea Ridge, Arkansas, on March 7, 1862, for all practicality established Federal control of the state of Missouri for the rest of the war.[7]

The story was the same in the Southwest, too. In July and August 1861, Lieutenant Colonel John R. Baylor led the 2nd Texas Mounted Rifles up the Rio Grande Valley into New Mexico. On August 1, he proclaimed the creation of the Confederate territory of Arizona (comprising what are today Arizona and New Mexico below the thirty-fourth parallel), with himself as governor.

In mid-December 1861, Brigadier General Henry H. Sibley marched into the territory with a Confederate army of twenty-six hundred. On February 21, 1862, he defeated a numerically stronger force of Federals under Colonel Edward R.S. Canby at Val Verde. Sibley next occupied Santé Fe, which had been evacuated by the Federals, who destroyed all the supplies they were not able to carry rather than have them fall into Confederate hands.

Events took a turn for the worse for the Confederates when most of their supply train was destroyed by the 1ˢᵗ Colorado Volunteers near Glorieta on March 28, 1862. Lack of supplies, a hostile population and news that Colonel James H. Carlton's two-thousand-man "California Column" was coming to Canby's rescue checkmated Confederate designs on New Mexico and Arizona. Sibley withdrew to San Antonio, and the Union army in New Mexico spent the rest of the war guarding the territory against Indian raids.

If the Confederates had secured the Southwest, they could have gone on to California, with its important ports of San Diego and San Francisco. They would also have had access to the gold and silver fields of California, Colorado and Nevada. Perhaps such clout would have yielded diplomatic recognition from England or France. But it just did not happen. And no other efforts were mounted by the Confederacy to take the Southwest.[8]

Thus, by the spring of 1862, one year after the war had started, the cancer of Union army occupation had started to eat away at sizable portions of the Confederacy. The Union dominated much of the Atlantic Coast, the border states of Maryland, Kentucky and Missouri, much of Tennessee and a large portion of the Mississippi River.

Despite the gloomy picture for the South, the situation would start to change in the summer of 1862. Out of the despair of defeat would come renewal. In the Deep South, morale was raised by the exploits of cavalry raiders John Hunt Morgan and Nathan Bedford Forrest. These "Wizards of the Saddle" completely disrupted the rail and communication lines of Union general Don Carlos Buell's army, forcing that commander to stop his offensive attack farther into the South.

In July, Morgan led his cavalry into Kentucky, calling for its citizens to "rise and arm, and drive the Hessian invaders" from the state. Meanwhile, Forrest and his cavalry captured an entire Union garrison at Murfreesboro, Tennessee. These raids were a national sensation, causing tangible damage to the Union war effort in the West and great consternation among Yankee authorities. In addition, they made Morgan and Forrest idols in the South and solidified the mystique of the Southern horseman.[9]

But it was in Virginia that the most dramatic morale-raising events took place. On May 31, 1862, Confederate general Joseph E. Johnston was seriously wounded at the Battle of Fair Oaks. In response, President Jefferson Davis appointed General Robert E. Lee to temporary command of the Army of Northern Virginia.

In response to the Union threat, Lee moved against McClellan's army on June 26, in what became known as the Seven Days' Campaign. Within a week,

McClellan was forced to withdraw his army from in front of Richmond to a position along the James River that was covered by the gunboats of the Union navy. Corresponding with this were Stonewall Jackson's acclaimed Valley Campaign, in which he defeated several Union armies, and a spectacular raid by Confederate general Jeb Stuart's cavalry around McClellan's army.

With McClellan neutralized, Lee soon led his army north, where he took on another Union force: Major General John Pope's Army of Virginia. With Major General Stonewall Jackson leading the way, Pope was forced to withdraw from his line along the Rappahannock River and move back toward Washington. Jackson even managed to march around Pope and destroy his supply base at Manassas Junction.

The decisive battle in the campaign, dubbed Second Manassas, took place on August 29 and 30. Pope's army was soundly defeated and retreated back to Washington.[10]

Therefore, by the late summer of 1862, things were looking up for the Confederacy. Perhaps the braggadocio was not empty after all. Maybe one Southerner was equal to ten Yankees in a fight. With these victories in mind, the Confederate high command began planning accordingly. What resulted was a series of mostly uncoordinated offensives on a thousand-mile front. In north Mississippi, a combined force under Confederate generals Sterling Price and Earl Van Dorn moved to retake the valuable rail center of Corinth. Around the same time, Braxton Bragg and Kirby Smith led columns into Kentucky, augmented by a smaller force under Brigadier General Humphrey Marshall. The goal here was to retake this border state for the Confederacy. Farther east, Confederate brigadier general William Loring led a small force into the Kanawha Valley of western Virginia (what was to become the state of West Virginia in June 1863) in hopes of bringing that part of the state back into the fold of the Confederacy.

Following his smashing victory at Second Manassas, Lee took the initiative, and on September 4, his army started crossing the Potomac at White's Ford. Feeling that he had the advantage over McClellan, he boldly split his army into several segments. Major General James Longstreet, in command of about ten thousand men, accompanied Lee toward Hagerstown on the Mason-Dixon line. This would be his springboard for invading Pennsylvania.

Three other columns under the operational control of Stonewall Jackson would encircle Harpers Ferry and force the surrender of that garrison of more than twelve thousand men. The division of General D.H. Hill would guard the South Mountain passes near Boonsboro, and Jeb Stuart's cavalry would scout the area for Union movements.

Eastern and Western Theaters of the war—late summer and fall, 1862. *Map by Steven Stanley.*

Victory was in no way apparent to the Union high command or to the Northern people during the first week of September 1862. With Lee's army in Maryland, a new Union force had to be literally reinvented to stop the Rebels. Major General George B. McClellan, a man who had failed Lincoln earlier that summer by failing to capture Richmond in the ill-fated Peninsula Campaign, was once again placed in command of an army being hastily assembled at Rockville, Maryland, just north of Washington. By September 13, most of this new Army of the Potomac was at Frederick, Maryland. There occurred one of the great flukes in U.S. military history. A copy of Lee's operational plan (the famous Special Order 191) for the opening phase of the invasion was discovered by some Union soldiers and made its way to McClellan. An ecstatic "Little Mac" gave chase and forced Lee—who had divided his army into five segments in order to capture the Union garrison at Harpers Ferry, as well as set the stage for a possible movement into Pennsylvania—to fight bloody holding actions in three of the South Mountain passes.

McClellan got his chance to beat Lee in the South Mountain passes on September 14, 1862. At Turner and Fox's Gaps, Confederate general D.H.

Maryland Campaign, September 1862. *Map by Steven Stanley.*

Hill's Division held off more than four times its number of Yankees until nightfall. Farther down the mountain range, a thin gray line of about fifteen hundred Rebels held up the Union Sixth Corps all day at Crampton's Gap. The Sixth Corps was to rescue the Union garrison at Harpers Ferry. At 7:15 p.m., Sixth Corps commander General William Franklin triumphantly sent a note to McClellan proclaiming:

> *The pass here is in our possession. The number of killed of ours is about 50, wounded about 200. We have about 120 prisoners. The loss of the enemy is greater than ours, but I cannot give it precisely. It has been a beautiful fight. Please send me orders as soon as convenient.*
> *Respectfully, WB Franklin*

General Robert E. Lee. *Library of Congress.*

But it was too late. Harpers Ferry would surrender the next day. In the largest surrender of U.S. troops until the fall of the Philippines in World War II, 12,737 men became prisoners of Stonewall Jackson. The Confederates also captured 73 cannons, 1,300 small arms and 200 wagons. Valuable foodstuffs such as 155,954 pounds of hard bread, 19,267 pounds of bacon, 1,545 pounds of salt beef, 1,315 pounds of salt pork and 4,903 pounds of coffee were also part of the booty garnered at Harpers Ferry.

The Battle of South Mountain marked the beginning of the end for Lee's invasion. The Federal pressure brought to bear there forced Lee to concentrate his forces at Sharpsburg, Maryland, near the Potomac, for a quick retreat back to Virginia. Lee contemplated such a move and only decided to stay and fight at Sharpsburg upon hearing the news that Jackson had captured Harpers Ferry and would soon be joining him with the rest of the army.[11]

By September 15, Confederate veterans of Turner's and Fox's Gaps, along with the remnants of Longstreet's column still at Hagerstown, were gathering around the village of Sharpsburg. With the news of Harpers Ferry's fall, Lee began to deploy his men along a meandering country stream called Antietam Creek.[12]

2

Two American Armies

The two American armies that clashed at Antietam were in their infancy in the fall of 1862. Both the Army of the Potomac and the Army of Northern Virginia would go on to greater glories on other fields. But in the Maryland Campaign, both forces would go through dramatic structural changes and challenges. To better understand what happened along Antietam Creek on September 17, a comparison of the armies—and their strengths and weaknesses—is in order.

General George B. McClellan was the thirty-five-year-old scion of a noted Pennsylvania medical family with roots going back to the *Mayflower*. Well schooled in military matters, he ranked second in the famous West Point class of 1846. His resume included experience both in the Mexican War and as an observer of European armies during the Crimean War. Nevertheless, his frequent caution in combat, coupled with his quarrels with Lincoln and his cabinet, proved to be his undoing as an army commander.

Like McClellan, General Robert E. Lee had aristocratic antecedents. His family was one of the first families of Virginia, and his father, "Light Horse Harry" Lee, was a hero of the Revolution. But this is where the similarities between the two men stop. Unlike his younger opponent, Lee was fifty-five years old at the time of the Battle of Sharpsburg. McClellan, in the prewar years, had left the army for lucrative work in the railroad industry. Lee, however, spent more than thirty years in the service. During this period, he was a cavalry commander, engineer on many of the Atlantic coastal fortifications, superintendent at West Point and an officer on the staff of General Winfield Scott in the Mexican War.

Major General George McClellan.
Library of Congress.

It was on Scott's staff where Lee gained valuable experience in how to lead an army. Whereas McClellan was often at odds with Lincoln and his cabinet, Lee had the full support of President Jefferson Davis and the Confederate Congress.[13]

The two armies that fought at Antietam represented a cross section of the American population. The soldiers on both sides were primarily from small towns or rural backgrounds. Union regiments claimed more urban enlistments. About one-fourth of the men in the Army of the Potomac were from New York. Pennsylvania represented the next largest group. Nearly 25 percent of Lee's army was from Virginia, with Georgia representing a close second, at about 21 percent. Although the Civil War is generally viewed as a conflict between white Anglo-Saxon Protestants, a close examination reveals an interesting ethnic makeup on both sides. To be sure, traditional groups such as the Scots-Irish and Pennsylvania Germans could be found in blue and gray. Many Southern soldiers from the Shenandoah Valley were of such backgrounds. They shared cultural, economic and kinship ties with the same groups in south central Pennsylvania. The influx of later emigrants from Germany and Catholic Ireland was very evident, particularly in the North. Units such as the Irish

Brigade and the German 5th Maryland (Union) and 20th New York served well at Antietam.

The famed Iron Brigade boasted Germans, Norwegians and Métis (men of French Canadian and Indian descent). Recent research by Iron Brigade scholar Lance Herdegen has uncovered the existence of at least two mulattos who passed for whites and were serving in the ranks. In recent years, the role of African Americans serving in the ranks of the Confederate army has been exaggerated. However, there are accounts of servants taking up arms alongside their masters in combat. And it would appear that a few could be found here and there serving in the Confederate army. For example, Charles Lutz, the son of a white father and mulatto mother, served in Company F, 8th Louisiana Infantry, and fought at Antietam. Lutz, however, was the exception rather than the rule.

Jews could be found in both armies. The 5th Maryland (Union), made up almost entirely of German immigrants, fought at Bloody Lane. Their commander was Major Leopold Blumenberg, a Jewish emigrant from East Prussia who had fled the Prussian army because of anti-Semitism. Settling in Baltimore, he upset many slaveholders because of his strong abolitionist stance. Among the Confederates opposing the 5th Maryland on the Sunken Road was the 12th Alabama. Captain Adolph Proskauer, another Jewish emigrant from Prussia, served with the 12th and was seriously wounded in the battle.

Even a solid Anglo command like the Texas Brigade had its minorities. Captain Decimus et Ultimus Barziza of Company C, 4th Texas, was the son of Italian immigrants. His name in Latin means "the tenth and the last" (apparently, his mother had had enough of child rearing when he came along).

Both Louisiana brigades in Lee's army were very cosmopolitan. Besides Louisiana French of both Creole and Acadian (Cajun) descent, the ranks were filled with men from all over the world. One study has shown that at least twenty-four nationalities were represented in these regiments, including Greeks, Italians, Mexicans, Brazilians and men from Martinique. The 12th South Carolina contained a number of Catawba Indians.

Hispanics could be found on both sides. The suffering of the 10th Louisiana was forever etched into history's memory when Alexander Gardner photographed the grotesque scene of the regiment's dead bodies along the Hagerstown Pike just two days after the battle. One of the dead in these photos may very well be Juan Tacon of Company G. A native of Mexico, Private Tacon was one of several dozen Hispanics in his company. Prior to enlisting, he had worked as a laborer in New Orleans. A number of other Spanish-surnamed solders of Company G were casualties that day. Another

Mexican, Private Anastasia Constantia, a shoemaker by trade, was captured and exchanged two months later. He was later wounded at Gettysburg. Lieutenant Severin Herrero had been at Malvern Hill in July, and at Antietam he suffered three wounds and was captured along the Hagerstown Pike. One of the wounds resulted in the amputation of his right arm.

Other Confederate units at Antietam had Hispanics on their rolls, particularly those raised in the Gulf States. For example, the 2nd and 8th Florida regiments, which fought at the Piper Farm in support of D.H. Hill's troops on the Sunken Road, had many Hispanics in their ranks. This was in no small measure because of Florida's long history as a Spanish colony. Company D of the 8th Florida had a large number of Hispanics, including officers, noncommissioned officers and enlisted men. Among them were First Sergeant Philip Gomez, Company D; Sergeant Andrew J. Acosta, Company F; and Second Lieutenant Julien Acosta and Private Joseph Hernandez, Company I. Lopez was a common name on the rolls of Company D. Perhaps these men were related. The names included Private Alfonzo Lopez, Sergeant Ignatio Lopez, Private Andrew M. Lopez Sr. and Second Sergeant Andrew M. Lopez Jr. The latter two names raise the question: how did Pop like taking orders from his kid?

Many Hispanics served with the Army of the Potomac, particularly in Massachusetts, New Jersey and New York regiments. Hispanic soldiers were part of the well-known 39th New York Infantry. Called the "Garibaldi Guards," the regiment was known for its distinctive uniform patterned after that of Italian elite troops known as the Bersaglieri. One company was composed of Spanish and Portuguese soldiers. This unit served in the Maryland Campaign and was captured by Stonewall Jackson, along with the rest of the Harpers Ferry garrison, on September 15, 1862.

The 48th Pennsylvania Infantry took part in the attack on Burnside Bridge. Later in the war, this regiment of miners from the coal country of western Pennsylvania went on to fame for digging the Petersburg mine. The architect of the plan to dig a tunnel under Confederate fortifications, pack it with some eight thousand pounds of gun powder and then blow it up was Colonel Henry Pleasants. At Antietam, he was a captain commanding Company C of the 48th. Three days after the battle, he was promoted to lieutenant colonel.

Henry Pleasants was born on February 17, 1833, in Buenos Aires, Argentina. His father, John Pleasants, was a native of Philadelphia and of Quaker stock. Henry's mother, Nieves Silviera, was Spanish. As a youth, Henry was educated in the Spanish and English schools of Buenos Aires. When he was thirteen, the family returned to Philadelphia, and Henry eventually studied civil engineering. He was working in the coal-mining region when the war broke out.[14]

McClellan's army was not the same force that had served in the Peninsula Campaign, nor was it the Army of the Potomac that would go on to glory at Gettysburg and other battles. At Antietam, McClellan had the Second, Fifth and Sixth Corps of his original Army of the Potomac. Two corps from Pope's ill-fated Army of Virginia were also in the fold. They became the First and Twelfth Corps. While the Eleventh Corps was kept back to guard Washington, the other two played key roles in opening the Battle of Antietam. The Ninth Corps comprised Major General Ambrose Burnside's unattached Carolina Expeditionary Force and the Kanawha Division from western Virginia.

The corps system was a Napoleonic innovation. The great emperor of France devised it as a miniature army containing three infantry divisions, artillery and cavalry. Such an organization provided simplification of command at the army level and flexibility in combat power. Such a force was designed to go forward and hold an enemy until the main army could arrive on the field. It was a major factor behind Napoleon's victories. Up to the time of the Civil War, the U.S. Army had been too small to adopt the corps system. With about sixteen thousand men scattered in posts on the frontier and along the coast, such an organization was not practical.

McClellan in Frederick, Maryland. *Library of Congress.*.

But by 1862, the corps had become the building block of the huge armies being raised by both sides.[15]

The quality of command and combat efficiency made the Army of the Potomac, numbering about 86,000, a patchwork force. The average Union regiment at Antietam had 346 men. Many of the new regiments had about 800 men.[16]

About one-fourth of McClellan's army was made up of raw recruits. These included "nine-month men," who were raised to cover the shortages caused by the War Department's premature and overoptimistic closing of recruiting offices that summer. Eighteen of these new regiments, about fifteen thousand men, became part of the army just prior to the march to Antietam. Another five thousand new recruits were added to the ranks of existing regiments as replacements. The nine-month regiments, as well as the replacements, lacked training and hindered the army by slowing it down on the march. Their ignorance of drill and firearms often proved fatal at the tactical level.[17]

McClellan's lieutenants were a mixed lot when it came to combat experience and competence. Half of his corps commanders were new to that level of command, including First Corps commander Major General Joseph Hooker. "Fighting Joe" was a West Point graduate and one of the most aggressive commanders on the field that day. Hooker had some great fighting units under his command, such as the famed Iron Brigade and the Pennsylvania Reserves. He also had some excellent combat commanders, such as Major General George G. Meade, who later commanded the army.

At sixty-five, Second Corps commander Edwin V. Sumner was the oldest active corps commander in

Major General George Gordon Meade. *Library of Congress.*

29

the Civil War. He had forty-three years of experience in the army, including several tours of duty in the West and distinguished service in the Mexican War. He led the Second Corps in the Peninsula Campaign, where he was wounded twice. At Antietam, his command was the largest on the field, with more than fifteen thousand men. This corps represented the best and the worst of the Army of the Potomac's combat efficiency. Major General Israel Richardson led the 1st Division. Nicknamed "Fighting Dick," this veteran of the Seminole and Mexican Wars was an aggressive commander. Conversely, the 3rd Division was commanded by Brigadier General William H. French, whose experience was as a brigade commander. Incredibly, this division had been put together on the march only sixteen hours before the battle. Nine out of its ten regiments had not seen any major combat.

Fitz John Porter, the Fifth Corps commander, had great potential from the start. The New Englander ranked eighth in his West Point class of 1845 and won several brevets for gallantry in the Mexican War. Later, he taught artillery at West Point and served in the Utah Expedition. On the peninsula, Porter led a division of the Third Corps and later the Fifth Corps. He had success at Mechanicsville, Gaines' Mill and Malvern Hill. Later, Porter and his corps were attached to the Army of Virginia just in time for the disastrous Second Manassas campaign. There, he was blamed by Pope for failure to provide proper support and was brought up on court-martial charges. Initially relieved of command, he was reinstated through the personal intercession of McClellan with President Lincoln. Many believe that the Fifth Corps could have been McClellan's weapon of final destruction against Lee at Antietam. But the two veteran divisions of Porter's command had suffered severe attrition both on the peninsula and at Second Manassas. A third division, under Brigadier General Andrew Humphreys, was on the march to reinforce Porter but arrived the day after the battle. Its combat effectiveness was dubious, since the entire division was made up of nine-month regiments.

Like Porter, Sixth Corps commander Major General William Franklin was also up on court-martial charges for disobedience at Second Manassas. Franklin had been trained at West Point as an engineer and graduated first in the class of 1843. But he lacked the aggression needed for combat operations. At Crampton's Gap on September 14, 1862, his trepidation resulted in the failure to raise the siege of Harpers Ferry. Conversely, at Antietam, he would unsuccessfully seek permission from McClellan to launch an attack against the Confederate left in the afternoon. Most of his men would not be engaged in the battle.

The foundation of the Union Ninth Corps at Antietam was Burnside's Expeditionary Force, which had successfully conducted amphibious operations in North Carolina during the first half of 1862. This unit returned to Virginia for Second Manassas and was augmented with Brigadier General Jacob Cox's Kanawha Division, which had been operating in the Kanawha Valley of western Virginia. On September 14, McClellan put his old friend Burnside in charge of the right wing of his army, consisting of the First and Ninth Corps, leaving Major General Jesse Reno in charge of the latter command. Upon Reno's death at South Mountain, Cox took over temporary command of the Ninth Corps.

The weakest link in McClellan's chain of command was Brigadier General J.K.F. Mansfield. This fifty-nine-year-old commander had an impressive military résumé. Ranking second in the West Point class of 1822, he spent his early military career constructing defenses of the southern coast. In the Mexican War, he won several brevets for gallantry and occasionally led troops in combat. In 1853, he was appointed to the staff rank of colonel in the inspector general's department, a position he held until the beginning of the war. When the fighting broke out, he spent most of his time on garrison duty. He arrived to command the Twelfth Corps two days before Antietam. This would be one of the few times he ever led men in battle, and the corps was the largest combat entity he had ever commanded.

The Twelfth Corps contained the largest component of nine-month regiments, five of them concentrated mostly in the 1st Brigade of the 1st Division. It was also the smallest corps in the army, fielding fewer than eight thousand men. These apparent deficiencies were offset by the presence of Brigadier General George S. Greene and his division—a seasoned command led by an experienced commander.[18]

As opposed to the patchwork combat quality of the Army of the Potomac, the Army of Northern Virginia was a lean fighting machine. This was an army of combat veterans. Lee's regiments were all battle-tested, and more than half had been in three or more major fights. Many of these soldiers had "seen the elephant" back in July 1861 at First Manassas. Twenty-two units had been in five battles. Only about 21 percent of the regiments had fought in just one battle. The Rebels were hardened veterans of First Manassas, Jackson's Valley campaign, Williamsburg, Seven Pines, the Seven Days' Battle, Cedar Mountain and Second Manassas. Their commanders were hardened veterans, too. Lee's chief lieutenants—Major Generals James Longstreet and Thomas J. "Stonewall" Jackson—led his two corps at Sharpsburg, although their commands were not officially designated as corps

Major General James Longstreet. *Library of Congress.*

until after the battle. That would require legislation from the Confederate Congress.[19]

The South Carolina–born Longstreet had a long military career that included combat in Mexico and against the Indians in Texas. He fought in many of the major conflicts of the Eastern Theater and was prominent in the Seven Days' Battle, where Lee dubbed him "the staff in my right hand." At Second Manassas, his troops launched the devastating counterattack that forced the withdrawal of Pope's army. At Sharpsburg, his command held the Confederate center and right.

Lee's infantry division commanders constituted an impressive array of combat leadership. Here was Major General John Bell Hood, a Texan via Kentucky, who was a virtual pit bull in battle. His aggressive leadership played a prominent role in preventing the collapse of the Confederate left on the morning of September 17. Soon after Hood's attack, the timely arrival of Major General Lafayette McLaws's Division helped wreck Major General John Sedgwick's division of Sumner's Second Corps. Another audacious commander in the campaign, Major General D.H. Hill, bought time for Lee at South Mountain, reinforced Jackson's flank in the West Woods and tenaciously held the Confederate center on the Sunken Road and at Piper Farm.

Jackson was Lee's other "wing" commander. This son of the western Virginia mountain region had earned his combat spurs early at First Manassas. His brilliant Valley Campaign in the spring of 1862 further solidified his greatness. His sluggishness in the Seven Days' campaign temporarily marred his reputation. However, he redeemed himself by capturing Harpers Ferry and holding Lee's left at Sharpsburg.[20]

It is believed that Lee had no more than 40,000 men at Sharpsburg. The months of campaigning and fighting had taken their toll. The average Confederate regiment numbered 166 men. Some had fewer. The 8th Georgia carried 85 officers and men into battle, while the 8th Virginia had 34 men and the 1st Louisiana Battalion numbered an amazing 17 combatants. At the other end of the spectrum, Longstreet's regiments averaged about 360 in the ranks, and the

Major General Stonewall Jackson. *Library of Congress.*

3rd North Carolina, recently augmented with conscripts, numbered 983.[21]

The official uniform coat of the U.S. Army was the frock coat. It was issued and worn by some units during the war. However, the average Union soldier at Antietam would have been clothed in the standard dark blue four-button blouse with light blue trousers. The blouse was also known as the sack coat. Its cut was based on the most popular civilian coat of the day, and it was issued by the army in 1858 for fatigue duty. The sack coat was very inexpensive to produce and was very comfortable. Although never intended to be worn in the field, its popularity with the average "Billy Yank" made it the unofficial standard uniform of the army. But within this sea of blue could be found a smattering of other hues and styles. Here was the Iron Brigade in frock coats and tall black hats; the 72nd Pennsylvania wearing short, Zouave-style jackets; a detachment of the 114th Pennsylvania, the "Collis Zouaves," attached to the 2nd Massachusetts, in the traditional turbans, short jackets and red baggy pants of the Zouaves; and the 1st and 2nd U.S. "Berdan's" Sharpshooters wearing coats of forest green.[22]

McClellan took great pains to see that his army was reequipped following months of campaigning. This took place at the camps at Rockville and through the establishment of supply depots at Frederick and Hagerstown, Maryland. Between September 12 and October 25, 1862, the army received more than 100,000 pairs of shoes and boots, 93,000 pairs of trousers 10,000 blankets and numerous other supplies.

This influx of supplies was not a mere luxury or crass display of Yankee abundance. They were sorely needed after all the hard campaigning that summer. For example, a few weeks after Antietam, the quartermaster of the First Corps was seeking more than five thousand shoes for the unshod soldiers of that command.[23]

The much-touted "ragged Reb" was in evidence during the Maryland campaign, perhaps more than in any other period of the war. Lee's men were particularly deficient in shoes, underwear and blankets. Numerous civilian eyewitness accounts bear this out. One Marylander observed, "They were the roughest looking set of creatures I ever saw, their features, hair, and clothing matted with dirt and filth." Angela Kirkham Davis, a Unionist citizen of Funkstown, Maryland, near Hagerstown, recalled, "They were tired, dirty, ragged and had no uniforms whatever. Their coats were made out of almost anything that you could imagine, butternut color predominating."[24]

A major cause of the ragged appearance of Lee's men was the inadequate supply system of the Confederate army. In the late summer of 1862, many Confederate regiments were still operating under the so-called commutation system of clothing supply. This system gave responsibility to each company commander for clothing his troops. The officer was to then seek reimbursement from the government. Individual Confederate states also undertook various measures to clothe their men, while private citizens got in on the act by raising money for uniforms. Meanwhile, the Confederate government was in the process of establishing quartermaster depots. However, it was not until late 1862 and early 1863, too late for Antietam, that Confederate authorities committed themselves to clothing their troops by direct government issue.[25]

Accordingly, a hodgepodge of uniforms was very much evident on the fields around Sharpsburg. Yet despite civilian accounts, the sparse photographic evidence that exists—mainly post-battle images of Confederate dead taken by Alexander Gardner—shows Confederates with short jackets, trousers and blanket rolls or knapsacks. Most of the men in these grim photos have shoes. Could it be that some of these troops, such as the dead Louisiana soldiers of Starke's Brigade, shared in the booty captured at Harpers Ferry on September 15? Perhaps. Most of these men got nowhere near the captured supplies there, however, since they were rushed to Sharpsburg for the battle. A rare image of Confederates in formation on the march, taken by a local photographer in Frederick, reveals what appear to be well-equipped soldiers wearing a wide variety of headgear. Historians are not positive whether this photo was taken in September 1862 or in July 1864, during Early's march on Washington.

Another interesting but inconclusive observation of Confederate uniforms was made by Union surgeon James L. Dunn in a letter to his wife after Antietam. He wrote, "All this stuff about their extreme destitution is all bash...I have yet to find a Rebel even meanly clad or shod. They are as well shod as our own men. They are dressed in gray."[26]

Counter to this was a letter from Major General Lafayette McLaws to his wife dated September 4, 1862. In it he states, "Many of our men are without shoes, and all of them are very ragged."[27]

Throughout the war, the Union infantrymen were usually better armed than their Rebel opponents. Antietam was no exception. The most common shoulder arm of the Yankee foot soldier was the Springfield rifle. This does not mean that there was not some degree of diversity of arms in the Union ranks. For example, some units such as the 7th West Virginia were armed with the British-made Enfield rifled musket. The 20th New York carried the U.S. Model 1841 Mississippi rifle with saber bayonet. The New York regiments of the Irish Brigade were issued the Model 1842 .69-caliber smoothbore musket. This was actually a favored weapon with the commander of the brigade, since it could fire "buck and ball" (a load of buckshot and musket ball) at close range with deadly effect.[28]

Correspondence sent from an ordnance officer in the Army of the Potomac to the chief of ordnance in Washington several weeks after the battle indicates that five thousand smoothbore muskets were still being carried by elements of McClellan's army. Esteemed Civil War weapons authority Joseph Bilby has stated that "as late as the battle of Gettysburg, July 1, 2 and 3, 1863, 10.5% of the regiments in the Army of the Potomac, the best equipped Federal army, were still armed, in whole or part, with obsolete smoothbore muskets." Bilby goes on to say that "except for their percussion ignition, these guns differed little in ballistic capability from the weapons shouldered by those Yankee soldiers' grandfathers in the Revolution and the War of 1812."[29]

The Confederate foot soldiers in Lee's army fielded a wider variety of weapons. These included several types of rifled muskets, such as the .577-caliber Enfield and the .58-caliber Springfield. Some of the men carried .54-caliber rifled muskets, including the U.S. Model 1855 Harpers Ferry rifle, the U.S. Model 1841 Mississippi rifle and the Austrian Lorenz rifle. Captured weapons, picked up on the battlefields of Virginia, helped alleviate Lee's deficit in arms. However, one estimate places the number of .69-caliber smoothbore muskets in the Army of Northern Virginia at about 30 percent. In the end, supplying the types of ammunition needed for these weapons was a logistical nightmare for the Confederate ordnance department.[30]

Although much is made of this lack of new weaponry, research shows that most of the opposing fire at Antietam was at a distance of about one hundred to two hundred yards, where smoothbore firearms were reasonably accurate. In his study of Civil War shoulder arms, Bilby mentions the work of British military historian Paddy Griffith, who asserted that the types of weapons used by the opposing sides in most Civil War battles mattered very little "because the tactics employed by officers on both sides led to essentially short-range firefights in which the accuracy of the individual or his weapon were largely irrelevant."[31]

Because of the destruction wrought by both armies' long arms, Antietam has aptly been nicknamed "Artillery Hell." The Army of the Potomac had the advantage both in quantity and quality. Reports of the number of Union guns engaged in the battle vary from 286 to 302. The main type of artillery in McClellan's arsenal was the twelve-pounder Napoleon, the workhorse of the army. There were 108 of these guns employed in the fight. Accurate up to one mile, they were also deadly when firing canister at shorter range. Napoleons were used en masse with awful effect to break up several Confederate attacks on the north end of the battlefield in the morning phase. A significant portion of the Union artillery consisted of state-of-the-art long-range rifled guns such as the ten- and twenty-pounder Parrott; 42 of the former and 30 of the latter pieces were brought to bear on the Confederate lines with deadly effect. Fifty-seven Union batteries were fielded on that bloody Wednesday.

Union artillery chief Henry Hunt wrote that, like other parts of McClellan's army, the artillery arm was "organized on the march" and in the intervals of conflict. In fact, Hunt had to reorganize the artillery just weeks before Antietam. Logistical problems existed, and many batteries were short of men, horses, guns and other equipment. McClellan had suffered losses on the peninsula, and Pope's disaster at Second Manassas included the loss of thirty guns captured by the Confederates. Hunt relieved many of these deficiencies within a very short time.

At Antietam, he still faced an organizational challenge. The batteries from elements of Pope's army were assigned to the corps. Conversely, McClellan preferred attaching three or four batteries per division. He redistributed the batteries to the divisions of the First Corps but left the Twelfth Corps with the system previously used under Pope. Essentially, infantry division commanders (and occasionally brigade commanders) had control of the artillery under them. About one-third of the Union batteries at Antietam were commanded by lieutenants. Accordingly, these lower-ranking officers deferred to infantry commanders for the tactical deployment of their cannons. Therefore, it was hard for the Union artillery to be massed at the tactical level, although in some cases this happened at Antietam on an ad hoc basis.

The Confederates had about 246 pieces of field artillery at Sharpsburg. The arsenal consisted of a hodgepodge of different model cannons, including 41 of the obsolete Model 1841 six-pounders. These Mexican War–era pieces were effective only at short range and threw a very weak punch. Lee had only 27 twelve-pounder Napoleons, and rifled guns were at a premium. In contrast to the Federals, the Confederates had only 4 twenty-pounder Parrott rifles and 36 of the ten-pounders. Compounding Lee's problems was the fact that of the fifty-nine batteries present, only five were uniform as to gun type. Lee was also bedeviled by inferior ammunition. A large number of fuses and shells exploded prematurely or not at all.

Like its Yankee counterpart, Lee's artillery was also in a state of reorganization. But like the rest of his command, the artillery of the Army of Northern Virginia was better organized for tactical application. Prior to Sharpsburg, Lee had assigned one artillery battalion, generally consisting of five or six batteries, to each of his infantry divisions. Longstreet's corps had a battalion attached to it. One for Jackson would come later. A reserve of four battalions and miscellaneous batteries was available for the army's general support. Despite the mixed quality of cannons, poor ammunition and other supply problems, Lee's artillery, as evidenced by Colonel S.D. Lee's Battalion near the Dunker Church, was still effective at massing guns and supporting the infantry.[32]

Cavalry played a limited role at Antietam. McClellan's horsemen were under the command of Brigadier General Alfred Pleasonton, a good bureaucrat but a poor field commander. Despite his prewar studies of European cavalry, McClellan also had little grasp of how to properly use his mounted arm. In an 1895 article in the *Cavalry Journal*, esteemed cavalry leader General Wesley Merritt wrote, "The cavalry under him [McClellan] was decimated instead of being concentrated, and each corps, division, and even brigade commander, was supplied with a force of this expensive arm, which necessarily reduced the available force of cavalry proper." Indeed, this parceling out of the cavalry diminished its field strength by about 17 percent.

But even if it had been properly utilized, the Union cavalry would have faced significant challenges. Many units were simply unfit for service. The 1st

Massachusetts Cavalry received no rations from September 2 to 20, leaving the troopers to fend for themselves on green corn, apples and the occasional generosity of local farmers. The regiment started the campaign seven hundred strong and within a few weeks after Antietam numbered fewer than three hundred men, many with uniforms in rags and without boots or stockings. In addition, the regiment did not have any tents. According to the regimental historian, the 3rd Pennsylvania began the march to Antietam as a "skeleton regiment." Most of the men had been sent to camp dismounted, and the remaining troopers were in a state "almost of destitution as regards clothing."

Despite deficiencies, by and large, McClellan's horse soldiers were better armed than their Southern opponents. Most of the Union cavalry regiments carried sabers, pistols and carbines, primarily the Model 1859 Sharps Breech-loading Carbine. The 3rd Pennsylvania carried many of the new models of cavalry carbines. McClellan chose to use the bulk of Pleasonton's cavalry to probe the Rebel center while dismounted on the skirmish line. On the north end of the field, units such as the 12th Pennsylvania Cavalry also served as provost guard, rounding up straggling infantry and forcing them back into the fight.

Most of the Union cavalry was deployed dismounted, used in a sort of "phony war" throughout the day, probing the Confederate center on the Boonsboro Pike.

In late July 1862, J.E.B. Stuart was promoted to major general and given command of a Confederate cavalry division consisting of three brigades. The Maryland campaign was the first time Stuart commanded such a large mounted force in the field. Lee's cavalry was indifferently armed—most troopers carried the standard U.S. Cavalry saber and pistol. A few companies had breech-loading carbines, more often than not captured from the Yankees. However, a large portion of Stuart's troopers carried the short Enfield rifle.

Major General J.E.B. Stuart. *Library of Congress.*

As was typical, particularly for this period of the war, the Confederate cavalry was used more aggressively at the tactical level. Stuart's cavaliers sparred with advance elements of the Union First Corps the evening before the battle and successfully guarded Lee's flanks on September 17. That afternoon, they were engaged in a failed reconnaissance in force against the Union right.[33]

Supplying and feeding an army has been a daunting task throughout history, and so it was in the Civil War. As would be expected, the Union had a huge edge in this category.

The men of the Army of the Potomac would arrive on the fields of Antietam well fed and well equipped. Soldiers received three pounds of rations per day. To carry food and forage, the army brought along more than three thousand wagons—each of which carried about a ton. This transportation system included more than thirty thousand horses and mules. Even with that support, much food was requisitioned from the local farmers, whether they were cooperative or not.

For the Confederates, the supply situation was acute. Lee had only about sixteen thousand horses of mixed quality and efficiency to pull his wagons. As previously noted, a lack of shoes along with a shortage of rations rendered some soldiers unfit to continue on the march into Maryland. Accordingly, thousands fell behind and did not catch up with the army until several days or even weeks after the battle.

Lieutenant Colonel Charles R. Sharder (U.S. Army ret.) has pointed out that "superior Union army logistics, or rather defective Confederate logistics, came close to deciding the contest at Antietam." However, McClellan's men were soon to find out that better uniforms, equipment and weapons were not all it takes to fight a battle.[34]

3

Sharpsburg and Environs

A "Tossed and Broken Sort of Place"

*A*ntietam is a Delaware Indian word meaning "swift flowing water." The creek is one of the major tributaries of the Potomac in the region. Its headwaters are located approximately thirty miles to the north at the base of South Mountain near the town of Waynesboro, Pennsylvania. The mouth of the Antietam is located about three miles south of Sharpsburg near the village of Antietam. There it flows into the Potomac River.[35]

Sharpsburg, Maryland, is located in what is known as the Great Valley. Geologically, the area is in the so-called Hagerstown Valley. Culturally, this area has been known as the Antietam Valley, Potomac Valley and Cumberland Valley. It is part of the Great Valley, which extends in a southwesterly direction from Quebec to Alabama. Approximately eight miles to the east is South Mountain, which is an extension of the Blue Ridge Mountains of Virginia. It is part of the Appalachian Mountain system of the eastern seaboard.

The soil in this area has a bedrock that is predominantly limestone. Outcroppings of limestone rock occur often in parallel lines, resulting in a pattern of pastures on rocky slopes and plowed fields on deeper soils. This abundance of stone was used by European settlers to construct stone wall fencing and to build farmhouses and barns. Indeed, this limestone was very evident in the town and noticed by visitors. In 1867, John T. Trowbridge visited Sharpsburg and noted it as "a tossed and broken sort of place, that looks as if the solid ground-swell of the earth had moved on and jostled it since the foundations were laid. As you go up and down the hilly streets, the pavements, composed of fragments of limestone slabs, thrust up such abrupt fangs and angles at you, that it is necessary to tread with exceeding caution" This limestone bedrock apparently serves as an aquifer due to the widespread occurrences of springs and a number of wells. In fact, the town of Sharpsburg was laid out around a water supply known as the "Great Spring," which can still be viewed today.[36]

Although the area, like most of the Great Valley, was shaded by climax forest, primarily oak and hickory, accounts suggest that at least parts of the Antietam Valley consisted of open plains with grass five or six feet high. It would take several generations of farming to clear this land. By the time of the Civil War, small woodlots were scattered about the area. Those such as what became known after the battle as the West Woods were managed woodlots. Farmers cut wood for firewood, fences and buildings, as well as to sell.

European settlers first arrived in the region early in the eighteenth century, and by then permanent Indian settlements in the area were almost nonexistent. However, tribes from both the north and south used the region for hunting, trade and as a corridor for war. Prehistoric archaeological data gleaned from the region suggests small group hunting camps. Indeed, hunting attracted Indians and Europeans since the area abounded with wildlife such as deer, bear, wild turkey and possibly buffalo. Today, visitors to Antietam National Battlefield may frequently see wildlife in the park. Deer, groundhogs, red foxes and other animals are common sights. This would not have been the case in 1862. Today, the National Park Service provides a protected sanctuary for these species. Back then, factors such as active farming, hunting and the presence of families, dogs and other farm animals would have kept the wild animal population under control. In addition, the white-tailed deer so often seen in the area today would be nearing extinction within a few years after the Civil War, only to be brought back by sportsmen later in the twentieth century.

In another piece, local historian John Smith wrote about a battle said to have taken place near Sharpsburg between the Delaware and Catawba tribes sometime in the 1730s. "The evidences of this conflict are still apparent in the skeletons which from time to time have been exhumed. Two years ago, when the break in the Chesapeake and Ohio Canal occurred at the Aqueduct and but a few steps from this battle ground, it became necessary to dig earth from this site to repair the break, when about two feet below the surface the workmen came across human skeletons, flints, arrow points, fragments of pottery and of pipes indicating that this was indeed the field of carnage." Some of the bones are now in my possession. Williams's *History of Washington County* relates a battle in 1736 between Delaware and Catawba Indians near the mouth of

Antietam Creek. While it is not obvious from Smith's description that this was a battle site, this is further evidence that these native peoples figured prominently in the early history of the area.[37]

Settlers arrived in the area in the 1730s and early 1740s, when the region was still part of Frederick County. In a sort of eighteenth-century version of the Homestead Act, Lord Baltimore issued a proclamation in 1732 offering settlers two hundred acres of land rent-free for three years and one-cent-per-acre rent annually in the fourth and subsequent years. Consequently, settlers poured over the mountains to the Antietam Valley.

Most of the settlers were German, with a few English and Scots-Irish. The Germans composed the major European ethnic group to settle the area. It is estimated that during the 1700s, about 70 percent of all German-speaking immigrants settled in Pennsylvania. From there, many migrated to western Maryland and Virginia's Shenandoah Valley. Accordingly, these German settlers are referred to as "Pennsylvania Germans." This is a broad term that includes immigrants from the Palatinate (sometimes called Palatines), Alsace/Lorraine on the French-German border and Switzerland. The German immigrants called themselves the "Deutsche," which was bastardized in English to "Dutch."[38]

A misnomer concerning the Germans is that they were all "sect people," members of the various Anabaptist sects such as the Mennonites and Dunkers. While it is true that the first sizable influx of Germans into Pennsylvania were Mennonites in 1716, these so-called sect people were a very visible minority in both Pennsylvania and western Maryland. The majority of Pennsylvania Germans were the so-called "church people"—Lutherans and Reformed.

The opening of lands in western Maryland proved beneficial to the colony. In 1745, Daniel Dulaney wrote to Governor Samuel Ogle, "You would be surprised to see how much the country is improved beyond the mountains, especially by the Germans, who are the best people that can be to settle a wilderness; and the fertility of the soil makes them ample amends for their industry." Another ethnic group that came over with the Germans were the French Huguenots. Some of the well-known families of Sharpsburg, such as the Prys and Roulettes trace their lineage to this heritage. While the origin of the term "Huguenot" is uncertain, it was first applied to French Protestants during the religious struggles of the sixteenth century. Religious persecution in France led to the dispersion of these people across Europe and around the world. Many Huguenots settled in parts of Germany and Switzerland and were amalgamated into those Germanic populations by the time of their arrival in the New World.

Sharpsburg and Environs

The first settlement of what became Sharpsburg consisted of four log cabins. Local tradition has it that one of these early structures was used for years as a trading post with the Indians. In 1755, British general Edward Braddock, accompanied by Colonel George Washington of the Virginia Militia and a mounted escort, passed through the hamlet en route to the ill-fated campaign against the French-held Fort Duquesne (present-day Pittsburgh). The British were slaughtered in an attack by French and Indian forces near the fort, and Braddock was mortally wounded. This defeat left the Pennsylvania, Maryland and Virginia frontiers unprotected and open to Indian attacks for several years during the so-called French and Indian War (Seven Years' War). In fact, because of this, the area remained largely unsettled until after that war.

Sharpsburg was founded in 1763 by Joseph Chapline, a member of a prominent Maryland colonial family, and named for Chapline's old friend, Maryland governor Horatio Sharpe. Later, Sharpsburg became part of Washington County after it was organized in 1776. Hagerstown and Sharpsburg are the oldest towns in the county. Both were formally laid out in 1763, although settlement existed there prior to that time. The first real store was kept by David R. Miller about 1768. He was the father of Colonel John Miller and grandfather of D.R. Miller of Cornfield fame.[39]

During this period of the eighteenth century, the village of Sharpsburg lay on the road to the Potomac and the ford at Mecklenburg (now Shepherdstown), Virginia. The latter location served the same purpose as places such as St. Joseph, Missouri, did for a later generation of pioneers. In the mid-1700s, areas such as the Shenandoah Valley and Kentucky were considered the "West." Thus, it is fair to assume that the small Maryland village played host to thousands of westward-bound families seeking water at the Big Spring or sustenance at a local tavern or trading post. An interesting anecdotal account of eighteenth-century Sharpsburg comes from Johann Conrad Dohla, a Hessian soldier. Dohla was taken prisoner at Yorktown and marched through the area to prison in nearby Frederick, Maryland, in 1782. His entry for January 30 states that after spending the night in Shepherdstown, they were marched over the frozen Potomac to Sharpsburg:

> *Today we marched only four miles, to Sharpsburg, a small place first developed fifteen years ago which is mostly settled by Germans. The leading citizen there is also the spiritual leader. Here we quartered in houses, and the inhabitants gave us food and drink, provided warm rooms, and showed us love and kindness, which improved our spirits.*

Because of its prominence during the colonial period as a community on the road to Virginia when Washington County was created in September 1776, Sharpsburg was up for consideration as the county seat. However, it lost out to Hagerstown by one vote. This shift in the base of political and economic power in the new county set the tone for the landscape at area farms for more than two centuries. Major highways, such as the National Road, and later railroads would come to Hagerstown, as it became a major center of population and commerce in the Great Valley. Conversely, Sharpsburg would remain a sleepy country town with limited population yet broad expanses of rolling farmland.

The opening up of lands west of the mountains by Lord Baltimore set the tone for settlement in the Antietam Valley. Soon, hundreds of settlers moved into the region. Sharpsburg was laid in 1763 and served as a commercial stop for settlers heading west. Thus, for a time, the village had potential as both a commercial and political center. This potential was lost when Hagerstown became the seat of government for Washington County, Maryland. Major transportation avenues would pass through the county seat, leaving Sharpsburg—in comparison to its thriving sister to the north—a somewhat small backwater community with plenty of open land for agriculture. As settlers cleared the land and erected stone wall fencing, they began the process of forever changing the surrounding terrain.

Despite losing the vote to have the county seat located there, Sharpsburg managed to sustain itself commercially as one of the major communities of southern Washington County. By 1820, the town population was 656. It contained at least three taverns, a post office, a market house, a fire company, two one-room schools and four churches. Fraternal organizations were an important part of nineteenth-century life, and in 1821, a Masonic Lodge was established there. Major crime in the area seems to have been occasional horse thieves and runaways. A reward of forty dollars was issued for a twenty-one-year-old runaway slave from nearby Bakersville. Conversely, the reward for a local shoemaker's apprentice who ran away was only ten cents.[40]

Transportation played an important role in the economy of Sharpsburg. In 1824, what became known as the "Middle Bridge" was completed east of town, taking the Boonsboro Pike across the Antietam. This was one of a series of multi-arch stone bridges built in the region around this time to cross Antietam Creek and other tributaries of the Potomac. Next, a stage line was established from Boonsboro to Winchester, Virginia, via Sharpsburg. Other stone bridges built during this era were the Hitt, or "Upper," Bridge (1830) and the Roherbach Bridge (Burnside, 1836). These structures facilitated

Postwar view of Main Street, Sharpsburg. *Antietam National Battlefield.*

agricultural commerce, providing farmers with easier access to the many gristmills in the area.[41]

Gristmills were the major agricultural business of the nineteenth century, and most millers ranked among the wealthy men of their community. Western Maryland, along with neighboring Pennsylvania and Virginia, was part of a wheat belt that made the region the nation's breadbasket. Indeed, much of the grain processed at mills in the Sharpsburg area made its way to the Port of Baltimore. From Maryland's premier city, wheat was shipped to ports all over the world. Therefore, it is not inconceivable that grain from the Sharpsburg area farms made its way to kitchens in such diverse places as Brazil and England.

By the 1830s, Washington County led the state in the value of its mills and the number of barrels of flour they produced. An important economic boon to the grain industry—and by far, the town—came in the late 1830s, when the Chesapeake and Ohio Canal was constructed nearby. Canal workers patronized local businesses, and many married local women and remained in the area. Local residents gained employment on the canal, and the waterway provided farmers with an avenue to ship flour and produce to markets in Georgetown. Even a number of canalboat captains made Sharpsburg their base, and for several generations canal work and farming were the main occupations for the citizens of Sharpsburg. By 1850, coal from the mines of western Maryland had become the canal's major product of transport. This was a high-grade bituminous, or soft, coal that was very much favored by transatlantic shipping companies. By the 1860s, more than 300,000 tons of coal were being shipped east on the canal. This made it a tempting target during all Confederate incursions north of the Potomac during the war.

A visitor to Antietam National Battlefield will notice that the park service has erected nineteenth-century-style wooden fencing along most of the tour road. This is but a fraction of what would have existed on the 1860s farmscape in the Sharpsburg area. Antietam National Battlefield cultural resource historian Keven Walker has pointed out that

> *a labyrinth of fences divided these areas for domestic use and helped maintain order and control over domestic life. In the 1800s, people fenced animals out versus today we think of fences as keeping animals in. This resulted in not only yard fencing designed to keep children out of wash yards and dogs and goats out of the garden but in miles and miles of fences around farm fields and wood lots and bordering almost every lane and avenue.*

A case in point was the farm of Samuel Mumma, who had fourteen fenced-in areas just for livestock. These fence systems became major obstacles for troop movements on September 17, 1862.[42]

The crops of that period looked much different from what is seen today in agricultural landscapes. Both field and sweet corn of a non-hybrid variety were grown, but because this corn was non-hybrid, there was no consistency. Stalks varied in height between six and fifteen feet and usually bore only one or two ears of corn. Prior to the use of chemical fertilizers and mechanized farm machinery, cornfields were planted in a "check row" pattern. The corn was planted at the intersection of these lines, resembling a checkerboard with two to four stalks per intersection, with the intersections placed about a yard apart. This spacing allowed a single horse and cultivator to run in any direction. During this period, it was not uncommon to see other crops planted amidst the cornstalks. These were typically pumpkins and pole beans. Other crops differed as well from their twenty-first-century varieties. Wheat, the major crop of the area, was also non-hybrid and was long stemmed and bearded. Plowed fields also had a different appearance, with deeper furrows than modern "no-till" operations.[43]

An architectural manifestation of farms at Antietam is the bank barn. Brought by the Germans, this is a two-story building. The first level was used for livestock, while the upper level was reserved for hay and grain. Confederate soldiers from the Deep South and frontier states such as Texas were in awe of these structures. For example, as members of Hood's Texas Brigade marched through Franklin County, Pennsylvania, about twenty-five miles north of Sharpsburg, one soldier noted that the barns were "more substantially and carefully built and fitted than any house…in Texas." He went on to write, "The barns were positively more tastily built than two thirds of the houses in Waco." After the Battle of Antietam, most of these barns served as field hospitals, and several were destroyed by fire during the battle.

One of the great landmarks of this rural landscape is the Dunker Church. The German Baptist Brethren, or "Dunkers," came out of a movement that began in Schwarzenau, Germany, in the early 1700s. The treaty that concluded the Thirty Years' War (1618–48) recognized three official state churches. Dissenters were persecuted and forced to seek sanctuary in places such as Schwarzenau, where some degree of toleration existed. The denomination was formed with the total immersion baptism of eight believers in the Eder River. The name "Dunker" derives from this form of baptism. They were pacifists and followed the biblical admonition, "Be not of the World." In the New World, the Dunkers first settled in Germantown, Pennsylvania. When western Maryland was opened to settlement, they, like their fellow Germans of the Lutheran and Reformed faiths, crossed the mountains and helped settle the Antietam Valley. For years, the small Dunker congregation met in the private home of Daniel Miller. In 1851, Samuel Mumma donated a four-and-a-half-acre plot of land on the western edge of his property for a church. The building was completed in 1853.[44]

Besides the church, many of the humble farmsteads at Antietam have taken the status of national landmarks because of their role in the battle. Accordingly, a review of their history and physical layout is appropriate for this study.

A number of these farms had slaves or free blacks who had been enslaved. At the time of the Battle of Antietam, there were a number of slaves or former slaves on area farms. Nancy Campbell was a freed slave living on the Roulette Farm and working there as a domestic servant. Jeremiah Summers was a thirteen-year-old slave on the Piper Farm. John Otto had two slaves. One was a fifty-four-year-old woman who very likely was a domestic. The other, Hilary Watson, worked alongside Otto in the fields and was hired out to other farmers.

At the north end of what was to become the battlefield lay the Joseph Poffenberger farm. This farm dated back to colonial days and was part of the original land patent of Sharpsburg's founder, Joseph Chapline. The farmhouse was probably built during the last half of the eighteenth century. During the 1830s and '40s, a barn and other outbuildings were constructed. Around 1850, Joseph Poffenberger and his wife, Mary Ann, acquired the property.

On the eve of the battle, Poffenberger's barn was full of wheat, flax, corn and clover, harvested that summer. A small orchard had yielded apples, peaches and plums, which Mary Ann had converted to preserves. The Poffenbergers also stored pickles, hundreds of pounds smoked meat and at least one barrel of whiskey. Chickens and horses were among Poffenberger's livestock. The latter were evacuated to safer areas on the eve of the battle. The Poffenbergers also sought safer climes on September 16. On the southern edge of the farm was a woodlot that became known as the North Woods. Composed primarily of oaks and walnut trees, this was one of three major woodlots that were key geographical features of the battlefield.[45]

Southwest of Poffenberger's farm was the Jacob Nicodemus farm. It consisted of a log house and a bank barn with a thatched roof made of rye straw. At the time of the battle, wheat was in stacks beside the farmyard, and there were sixteen

Image believed to be the Poffenberger family on the front porch of their farmhouse. *Western Maryland Room, Washington County Free Library, Hagerstown, Maryland.*

acres of corn. Although not as extensive as neighboring farms, Nicodemus had his share of livestock, too. More than thirty pigs roamed the fields and nearby woods. He also had over twenty head of cattle and six horses. The hill on the Nicodemus land would forever be etched into history as Nicodemus Heights, the position of General J.E.B. Stuart's artillery at the outset of the battle.

A short distance south of Poffenberger's was the D.R. Miller farm, its barnyard surrounded by large haystacks. This was another property originally part of Chapline's tract. David R. Miller moved there almost twenty years before the battle. His father, Colonel John Miller (the "Colonel" was a militia rank from the War of 1812), was a wealthy landowner who financed the purchase of farms in the area for all of his sons.

The Miller house sat on a small rise facing south, just opposite the Hagerstown Turnpike. The exterior was stucco, cut to resemble stone. Large walnut trees stood around it, whitewashed as a protection against pests. An arbor contained grapevines. The house, originally a log structure, had been

D.R. Miller's Farm. *From* Antietam Farmsteads.

built about 1800. Various outbuildings were on the property, including a blacksmith shop and a springhouse next to the road. The Miller barn, stable, corncrib/wagon shed and hog pens were located on the west side of Hagerstown Pike. A whitewashed stone wall lined the road on both sides.[46]

A short distance south of Miller's was the Samuel Mumma farm. This property was composed of parts of three colonial land grants. The Mumma farmhouse and some outbuildings were built in the eighteenth century. On the eve of the battle, the Mumma Farm and environs were typical of the prosperous farmlands of the area. Out of the 150 acres on the site, 120 were improved with a cash value of $11,000. Just prior to the outbreak of the war, Mumma had further diversified his agricultural operations, with wheat and corn being his principal crops. Traveling from the Smoketown Road via Mumma Lane, one would have first noticed the solemnity of the family cemetery just to the north and surrounded by a paling fence. A few yards farther on, a visitor would be greeted with the sight of at least seven shade trees (possibly walnut trees)[47] on the south side of the lane, marking the entrance to the farmstead proper. Beyond those trees, a little farther south, were four large haystacks. Trekking on toward the farmhouse, you would notice just to the north a corncrib and wagon shed. To your right, on the south side, would be about ten fruit trees, perhaps cherry. These bordered the lane and a large garden. Near the southern end of the garden were two outbuildings. One would see a stove, sausage grinder and stuffer and a lard press, among other appliances.

Across from the house was another garden. The gardens at Mumma would have yielded a variety of produce. Closest to the farmhouse were probably grown herbs, spices and perhaps certain medicinal plants. Records indicate that "Irish potatoes" were a major garden crop with an annual yield of about seventy-five bushels. Sweet potatoes were a possible other crop. Much of both gardens was probably surrounded by a whitewashed paling fence approximately five feet high.

Beyond that garden was the massive bank barn, so typical of the region. In or around this structure would be found state-of-the-art farm equipment of the mid-nineteenth century, such as a McCormick reaper and a threshing machine. Other tools found in this area included plows, wheat drills and grain rakes. Inside the barn, eighty bushels of wheat, twenty of rye and twenty-five of corn were stored. Somewhere near the barn is very likely where Mumma kept his pig pen. This included more than a dozen large hogs, along with probably that many "shoats" (young hogs weighing between 100 and 180 pounds). Behind the barn was a large apple orchard containing more than forty trees. Walking back to the farmyard, you would notice several smaller trees, some of them probably cedar, in the yard behind the house. They surrounded a larger hardwood tree, maybe a walnut. Around these trees in the farmyard, you would probably see chickens, turkeys and ducks. In one of the outbuildings, or perhaps on the back porch of the house, would have been a supply of cordwood. Mumma had cut 295 cords of wood. Twenty cords were for his personal use, and the remainder was to be sold for upwards of four dollars per cord. Mr. Mumma owned at least two wagons, and one of them would have been used to haul wood from lots on his land.[48]

One of the more impressive farmsteads was owned by William Roulette. Originally a log house built before the French and Indian War, the house was constructed in stages through the late eighteenth century and into the first decades of the nineteenth century. Like other farms, it went through several owners. Roulette was the grandson of a French Huguenot immigrant to Washington County. He had fathered seven children ranging in age from infant to eleven years old. At the war's outbreak, he held 198 acres valued at $9,000. This included eight horses, fourteen head of cattle, eleven sheep and twenty hogs. He produced wheat, rye, corn, oats, hay, wool, Irish potatoes, butter and honey. He also had a small orchard. A sunken farm lane traversed the southern edge of the farm. It was known locally as "Hog Trough Road." Soon, it would take on a more ominous name: "Bloody Lane."[49]

On the southern edge of Hog Trough Road was the 231-acre Piper Farm. The circa 1820s farm had a hewn log farmhouse with a shingled roof and stone chimney. A white picket fence surrounded the house and yard. Henry Piper purchased the place from his father in 1854. A small barn and six other outbuildings, including slave quarters for the several slaves owned by Piper, completed the physical plant there. Like his neighbors, a major crop for Piper was corn. Thus, this crop covered the field due north of the house up to the Hog Trough Road. The fields to the east were plowed, and those to the south and

William Roulette. *Philip Roulette Collection.*

west were either stubble or grass in September 1862. Piper also had a forty-eight-thousand-square-foot orchard surrounded by paling fence between the house and the cornfield. This was the largest orchard in the area and a commercial orchard as well. It was rare for this period of history, since large commercial orchards did not come about in the region until the latter part of the nineteenth century.[50]

To the east of Sharpsburg, straddling the Boonsboro Road at Antietam Creek, was the Joshua Newcomer farm. At the time of the war, this was a bustling site complete with gristmill, sawmill, plaster mill and other workshops, dating back to the colonial period. A stone bridge stood adjacent to Newcomer's. After the battle, it became known as "Middle Bridge." A small dam just downstream on the Antietam facilitated water flow into Newcomer's millrace. Parts of Newcomer's property and building may be seen in several photographs of the Middle Bridge, taken after the battle by photographer Alexander Gardner.[51]

About one mile to the east, just north of the Boonsboro Road, was the farm of Philip Pry. Another local citizen with French Huguenot antecedents, Philip inherited the farm from his father and, in 1844, constructed the imposing brick farmhouse that would serve as General George B. McClellan's headquarters during the Battle of Antietam. Here, Pry lived and farmed with his wife, Elizabeth, their six children and a nineteen-year-old slave named Georgiana, who assisted Mrs. Pry with domestic chores.[52]

Moving back to Antietam Creek and downstream were two farmsteads that were key landmarks during the afternoon phase of the battle. The original farmhouse owned by Joseph Sherrick and dating to the late 1700s was log. In the 1830s, a large brick house replaced it. Sherrick, whose roots went back to colonial Pennsylvania, was a member of the local Dunker congregation. By the time of the battle, it appears that he had moved to another locale and was leasing the farm to Leonard Emmert.

Just across the road from Sherrick's was the farm of John Otto. The Ottos were one of the oldest families in the Sharpsburg area. In 1833, John purchased the farm that bears his name. At the time of the battle, Otto's farmhouse was painted a light blue. Over the years prior to the battle, the obligatory outbuildings and fencing were constructed on the site. These included a log kitchen behind the house, a storehouse for food built into a nearby hill, a bank barn and a hog pen. A white paling fence surrounded the family garden, and nearby fruit trees yielded apples and pears. Here, Otto lived with his wife, children and two slaves. Like his neighbors the Sherricks, Otto was a Dunker. In fact, the bricks for the Dunker Church were made at the Otto Farm and donated to the congregation.[53]

4

Prelude to a Bloodbath

On September 15 and 16, Lee gathered his scattered forces from the vicinity of Hagerstown, Boonsboro and Harpers Ferry, positioning his troops on Sharpsburg Ridge and west of Antietam Creek, running north and south parallel to the Hagerstown Turnpike. This well-maintained road led to the county seat of Hagerstown, twelve miles to the north. Another five miles farther north was the Mason-Dixon line and across that, Pennsylvania. Lee was close, yet so far away from one of the goals of his invasion. During the battle, this road provided Lee with what is known in military parlance as good "interior lines." In other words, he could move troops and artillery up and down the road relatively unobstructed and much more quickly to reinforce parts of his line on the northern half of the battlefield.

Lee's left was under the operational control of Jackson, and the center and right were under Longstreet. By the morning of the battle (September 17), Lee had about twenty-five thousand men to face his opponent. As troops arrived that day from Harpers Ferry, they were fed into the battle, and Lee eventually had nearly forty thousand men on the field. McClellan had about eighty-six thousand men. Of these, about sixty-five thousand were committed to the battle.

In the early morning fog of September 16, McClellan directed his artillery chief, Henry Hunt, to deploy his reserve artillery on the bluffs east of the creek overlooking the Middle Bridge. Soon, an artillery duel ensued, with the opposing and greatly outgunned Confederate batteries to the west. Confederate participation in this affair was short-lived. Their batteries were low on ammunition and could not compete with Union rifled cannons.

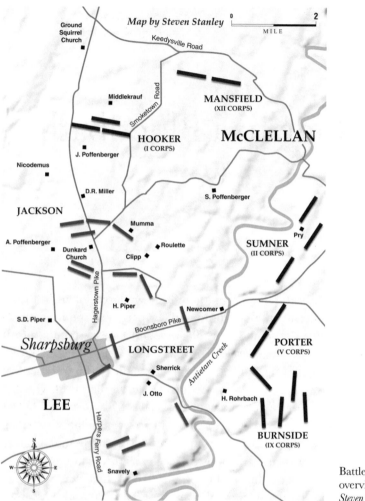

Battle of Antietam, overview. *Map by Steven Stanley.*

Accordingly, Longstreet directed both artillery and infantry in the area to take cover behind Sharpsburg Ridge.[54]

However, some of the Rebel cannons found their mark. One soldier with the 8th Ohio wrote an account that was a portent of the bloodshed to come. His unit was on line supporting the Union batteries on the bluffs overlooking Antietam Creek:

I was standing about ten paces from the center of the Regiment and directly opposite the colors, as I saw a twelve pound conical coming. It was directly in line of the regiment, and I was wondering who of our number must go now, as it approached the colors and fell among a little group, who were sitting by them. A little cloud of dust enveloped them as they sprang to their feet. It cleared away and I saw that one had not risen. Poor Farmer, one of the color guard, lay quivering in death. The shell had not burst, but rebounding it tore away the right and lower part of his side then fell by its victim unconscious of its fatal effects. A little party of his comrades gathered around as with a few shuddering groans poor Farmer slept the sleep of death while the wind rustling through its silken folds, seemed to make the old flag droop and sigh for its brave guard, unable to defend it longer. [55]

Meanwhile, a little after 7:00 a.m., elements of the 3rd and 4th U.S. Infantry sparred with Confederate skirmishers at the Middle Bridge. After a brief flurry of musketry, the Confederates fell back, and the Union troops held the bridge. Later, sometime after noon, elements of the Union Ninth Corps were sent downstream to the Rohrbach or Lower Bridge (soon to be dubbed the Burnside Bridge). One company of the 30th Ohio drove a skirmish line from Brigadier General Robert Toombs's Georgia Brigade back across the creek, securing the area east of the bridge for the Union forces. [56]

That afternoon, McClellan directed the First Corps under Major General Joseph "Fighting Joe" Hooker to move across Antietam Creek via the Hitt or Upper Bridge. He was to be supported by General J.F.K. Mansfield's Twelfth Corps, which marched out late on the sixteenth. Hooker's order were to strike Lee's left along Hagerstown Road less than two miles north of Sharpsburg. The next day, the Second Corps, under Major General Edwin V. Sumner, was to lead his command across the creek to assist in the destruction of the Confederate left flank. Eventually, the Union Sixth Corps would also march to this sector on the afternoon of the seventeenth. Many historians have criticized McClellan for "signaling his punch" by sending Hooker and Mansfield to this sector on the sixteenth. However, this movement caused Lee to shift a large portion of his army to that part of the field, weakening his center and right flank. Also, Hooker's blocking of the Hagerstown Pike seriously restricted Lee's movements and possibly closed the final door of opportunity to move north to Hagerstown and beyond.

To this day, McClellan's battle plan appears complicated and confusing. Besides sending the above-mentioned commands against Lee's left, the Ninth Corps was to go against Lee's right if feasible. If either of these attacks were to be successful, the option would be open to strike Lee's center with two corps held in reserve—the Fifth and Sixth—along with the cavalry of the Army of the Potomac. Any tactical combination thereof would drive the Rebels into the Potomac and quite possibly end the war. McClellan's instructions to his corps commanders were often ambiguous, and he never got them together for a council of war. As a result, from the Union perspective, the Battle of Antietam quickly devolved into a battle of uncoordinated piecemeal assaults, often at the regimental or brigade level. This would allow Lee the opportunity to use his excellent interior lines via the Hagerstown Pike to shift troops back and forth to meet the various Union threats.[57]

As McClellan's men marched into position, things were busy in the Confederate lines, too. Early on the sixteenth, most of Brigadier General Fitzhugh Lee's cavalry brigade was in the fields around the Dunker Church. Also, detachments were deployed in advance on the Hagerstown Road and on the Smoketown Road to the east, observing the crossings of the Antietam.[58] That day, the 9th Virginia Cavalry passed the church and rode east on Smoketown Road to the East Woods in order to support a section of Pelham's battery and to reconnoiter Union movements. In the afternoon, General John B. Hood's Division, Longstreet's Command, took position "near the Hagerstown pike, in an open field in front" of the Dunker Church." In his official report, Hood erroneously referred to the church as "Saint Mumma Church." The bulk of his command remained here until about sunset.

Both Hood and Lee's cavalry chief, General J.E.B. Stuart, was at the church when vedettes came in and reported Union columns crossing at the Upper Bridge and the Pry Ford. From here, Stuart dispatched Fitz Lee's Brigade, and Hood sent elements of the 2nd Mississippi, 6th North Carolina and 4th Texas first to the vicinity of the East Woods. Other Confederate troops from D.H. Hill's Division were deployed as skirmishers to support this movement. Artillery from several batteries was also brought up.[59]

The Rebels were opposing advance elements of Meade's Division of the Union First Corps: the 3rd Pennsylvania Cavalry, 3rd Pennsylvania Reserves, Magilton's Brigade and 13th Pennsylvania Reserves (Bucktails), Seymour's Brigade. About sunset, Hood's entire division moved forward from the church in support, it's right flank skirting the Mumma Farm. Soon, the rest of Seymour's Brigade—the 1st, 2nd, 5th and 6th Pennsylvania Reserves—along with several Union batteries, moved forward to reinforce the Bucktails. Meanwhile, Meade sent the rest of his division, the brigades of Magilton and Anderson, west onto the Joseph Poffenberger farm, driving Confederate skirmishers out of the North Woods

Although the opposing sides exchanged small arms and artillery fire for several hours in the vicinity of the East Woods and Miller's Cornfield, losses on either side were not heavy. The affair was more bombast than anything else. Confederate major H.J. Williams of Winder's Brigade wrote of the Yankee cannon fire, "The display was grand and comparatively harmless, except to the stragglers in [the] far rear." However, there were casualties on both sides. One of the first to fall was Colonel Hugh W. McNeil, commander of the Bucktails. He fell with a rifle ball to the heart while leading his men at the start of the action. On the Southern side, Colonel P.E. Liddle, commander of the 11th Mississippi, was mortally wounded by a stray round as he watched the action from the rear several yards from the fighting. One of the more gruesome casualties was incurred in the 9th Louisiana of Jackson's Division (J.R. Jones commanding), which arrived to support Hood. Near dark, Lieutenant A.M. Gordon, acting adjutant of the regiment, was killed by a Union shell that cut off both his legs at the thigh.[60]

While Hood was engaged, General Thomas J. "Stonewall" Jackson arrived on the field with his old division now led by Brigadier General J.R. Jones. It was followed by the division of Brigadier General A.R. Lawton. Both commands marched past the Dunker Church and deployed to the north and west, opposite Hagerstown Road, with two brigades—Lawton and Trimble—held in reserve near the church. Around the same time as Jackson's arrival, Stuart's cavalry fell back and "for a time rested in the fields east of the church."[61]

About 9:00 p.m., a reconnoitering party from the 5th Pennsylvania Reserves was sent forward from the East Woods. This twenty-four-man detachment led by Lieutenant H.P. Petriken exchanged fire with elements of the 4th Alabama and 6th North Carolina. In the brief firefight, Petriken was mortally wounded and left on the field to the mercy of the Confederates. Some of the men from the 4th Alabama took him to the Dunker Church, where he was "tenderly cared for, but died that night. His watch was returned to his family by Captain W.M. Robbins of the 4th Alabama."[62]

About 10:00 p.m., Hood received permission from Jackson to withdraw his division to a position about two hundred yards behind the Dunker Church. This was to allow his men to cook their rations. The dawn would bring some of the worst carnage ever seen on the North American continent.

Tens of thousands of soldiers, Americans all, slept as best they could that night. An unknown soldier in the 5th Alabama penned words home to his parents that evening that perhaps reflected the feelings of many soldiers:

My Dearest Parents,

I never could fully appreciate all the blessings of a good home until I entered camp. So were it not for the consolation of religion I do not know how I should be able to bare [sic] *up under it, but whenever I feel oppressed I fly to my Bible and there can always find consolation; dear Mother, you do not know how much I have been comforted from the dear little Bible you gave me when I left home, and how much I have thought of your parting advice.*[63]

The young Alabamian was surely not alone in his thoughts of home and the need for prayer.

5

Cornfield and East Woods

The battle began at about 5:15 a.m., with the stars still in the sky in the early morning mist, as Union and Confederate artillery commenced firing and Hooker ordered advance elements of his First Corps to move south parallel to the Hagerstown Pike. Nobody is positive who fired the first shots, but years later Lieutenant Asher Garber of the Staunton (Virginia) Artillery recalled that his guns on Nicodemus Heights "opened the fight." Soon, the air filled with missiles as counter-battery fire erupted between Pelham's guns and the Yankees on Poffenberger Farm. Union battery commander J. Albert Monroe recalled, "The opposite hill seemed suddenly to have become an active volcano, belching forth flame, smoke and scoria." One of the first Confederate rounds cut the throats of two horses in Edgell's New Hampshire Battery. Soon, at least twenty-four Union cannons were replying to the Rebel gunners with deadly accuracy.[64]

The constant rain of artillery shells would have been unnerving to the average soldier. D.C. Love of Company E, 11th Mississippi, wrote home to his wife that after rations were distributed early that morning, the shelling of the West Woods began. He went on to say that a shell fragment struck a soldier in the nearby 4th Alabama Infantry, and it "threw a section of his skull" into the ranks of the Mississippians. No doubt such an incident did little to calm the fears of nervous soldiers waiting to go into combat.

A tradition of the Battle of Antietam is that Pelham, with about fifteen guns, held Nicodemus Heights, anchoring Lee's left, all day. In reality, the heavy Union counter-battery fire from the more than forty massed cannons of the Union First Corps was a major cause for the "Gallant

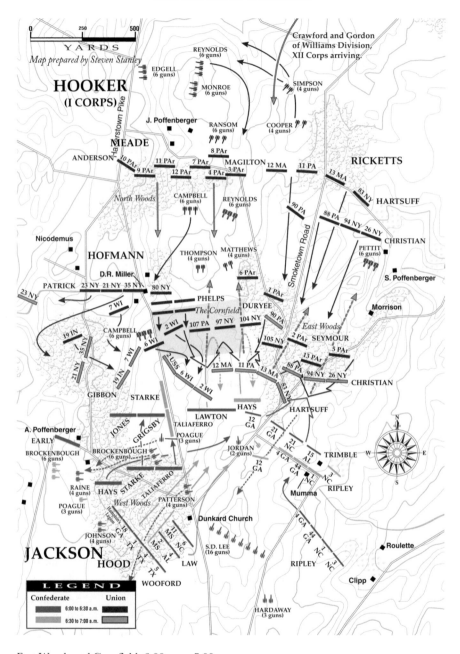

East Woods and Cornfield, 6:00 a.m.–7:00 a.m.

Pelham" to withdraw to safer parts of the field within ninety minutes of the start of the battle.[65]

One question remains unanswered regarding Nicodemus Heights. When the Confederates withdrew their guns, why didn't Hooker move troops to occupy the commanding eminence? Other Confederate artillery, about sixteen guns of Colonel S.D. Lee's Battalion, on the high ground east of Dunker Church, poured a galling fire into the Union infantry advance that bloody morning. Counter-battery fire from Hooker's guns at Poffenberger's and from

Major General Joseph Hooker. *Library of Congress.*

long-range rifled twenty-pound Parrot pieces massed by Union artillery chief Henry Hunt east of the Antietam made S.D. Lee's position untenable by 8:45 a.m. In his own words, Lee described his artillery battalion as "pretty well wrecked," with losses of more than eighty men killed or wounded out of three hundred engaged, as well as sixty horses lost. This was a very heavy toll for an artillery command in the Civil War.[66]

Forming the right of Hooker's First Corps, Doubleday's Division, including the soon-to-be-famous "Iron Brigade," moved out along the Hagerstown Pike. Meade's Division, composed of the Pennsylvania Reserves, held the center rear, poised to go to the support of Doubleday or Rickett's Division on Hooker's left flank.[67]

The opposing infantry made contact in the East Woods about 5:30 a.m. At that time, Lieutenant Colonel Truman Seymour's nine-hundred-man-strong brigade of Pennsylvania Reserves began to spar with Jackson's right. Seymour, a native of Vermont, was a combat veteran of both the Mexican and Seminole Wars. An accomplished artist, he taught drawing at West Point for a time. After a long career in the army, he retired to Florence, Italy, where he spent the rest of his life doing watercolors.[68]

Brigadier General Truman Seymour. *Library of Congress.*

It had been an uneasy night for the Pennsylvanians, and most of the men had little or no sleep. This was coupled with the fact that they were weary from the combat at Turner's Pass three days earlier and from the skirmishing the night before with Hood's Division. Indeed, the Pennsylvanians had been trading shots with the Rebels on the skirmish since three o'clock that morning.

Opposing them were seven hundred gray coats of Trimble's Brigade, now under the command of Colonel James A. Walker. The thirty-year-old Virginian was descended from some of the earliest Scots-Irish settlers of the Shenandoah Valley. Walker's Celtic temper got the best of him during his senior year at Virginia Military Institute (VMI). There he squabbled with then professor Thomas J. Jackson and challenged him to a duel. Although he ranked high in his class, Walker was court-martialed and dismissed from VMI. Walker went on to teach school for a time and work for a railroad before going on to the University of Virginia, where he got his law degree.

Early in the war, he was promoted to lieutenant colonel of the 13th Virginia Infantry and eleven months later became its colonel. His fearlessness in battle earned him the nickname "Old Bull Dog" by his men and the respect of his old nemesis Jackson.[69]

In the vicinity of the East Woods, Rickett's Yankees traded shots with Rebels in that sector for about an hour. A charge by one his brigades, led by Abram Duryea, was shattered by Confederate musketry. In less than thirty minutes, Duryea lost a third of his command. Duryea's repulse was due in large part to the lack of support from Rickett's other two brigades, Hartsuff and Christian. Both of their advances got bogged down for different reasons.[70]

Brigadier General George L. Hartsuff was a veteran of the Seminole War, during which he received two very serious wounds. Now at Antietam, he halted his brigade and rode forward to reconnoiter. Soon, he was seriously wounded by a shell fragment and carried from the field. Hartsuff's wound left him disabled for many months. His wounding caused about a thirty-minute delay as his successor, Colonel Richard Coulter of the 11th Pennsylvania, grappled with the reins of command. Hartsuff's Brigade was cut to pieces as it moved forward against Confederate artillery and musketry. In less than half an hour, many of his regiments simply dissolved.[71]

Brigadier General George L. Hartsuff. *Library of Congress.*

The 12th Massachusetts carried 334 officers and men into the fight. In this brief period, they lost 49 killed, 165 wounded and 10 missing for a total of 224—a stunning loss of 67 percent. Regimental commander Major Burbank was mortally wounded, and the color guard of the 12th was practically wiped out. The 11th Pennsylvania suffered a similar fate, losing more than half its men in the fighting. Some were luckier than others. Private Prince A. Dunton, Company H, 13th Massachusetts, wrote to a friend a few days after the battle, "One ball just grazed my shoe. The men that stood each side of me got shot. I do not see how any of us got out alive."[72]

Brigade commander Colonel William H. Christian led his men forward under Confederate artillery fire. Christian apparently went into shock and began to drill the brigade under fire as if it were on the parade ground. Finally, he fled the field in panic when Rebel cannon shells began bursting in the treetops above him. Later, he was seen cowering behind a tree. William Christian was never able to overcome the shame of his battlefield performance at Antietam. That evening, Rickett asked for and got Christian's resignation.

Colonel James Washington Jackson, commander of the 47th Alabama Infantry. *Antietam National Battlefield.*

Plagued by depression in the postwar years, he died in an insane asylum twenty-five years later. The loss of these two left a temporary command control void that cost valuable time and hindered Rickett's advance.[73]

A bold counterattack by Harry Hay's "Louisiana Tigers" further frustrated Union movements in this sector and bought time for Jackson. Tennessee-born Hays was a New Orleans lawyer and prominent political figure at the outbreak of the war. A hard- charging and hard-drinking commander, he had led Louisiana troops from the start, at battles such as First Manassas and Port Republic. He received his brigadier general's star on July 25, 1862.

His was one of two brigades in Lee's army bearing the generic title "Louisiana Tigers," a sobriquet derived from a New Orleans–based rifle company formed early in the war. Hay's brigade suffered some of the heaviest losses in this sector. Out of 550 engaged, 323 were casualties, including every regimental commander and their staff.[74]

As the Confederate lines crumbled in the Cornfield area, Louisiana once again did itself proud. This time, it was the brigade of Brigadier General William Starke, who ascended to the command of Jackson's Division when J.R. Jones, who gained a reputation as a poltroon during the war and was cashiered from the army in 1863 for cowardice, left the field after being too close to a Yankee cannon shell that exploded nearby. Forty-eight-year-old Virginia native William E. Starke had been a successful businessman in Mobile and New Orleans prior to the war. When his native state seceded, he returned there, saw service in some of the early campaigns of the war and was commended twice for gallantry in the Seven Days' Battle before Richmond. Starke was promoted to brigadier general and placed in command of the Louisiana Brigade. This caused resentment in the ranks, as the Louisianans felt that one of their own colonels should have been placed in command. Thus, Starke bore the responsibilities of combat command and the added burden of having to prove himself to his officers and men. His chance for redemption came at Second Manassas, where he seized the brigade colors and personally led a successful counterattack, driving the Yankees from the battlefield. Respect for Starke in the ranks grew when he stood up to "Stonewall" Jackson himself over a question of whether some of his men had robbed civilians in Frederick, Maryland. Although, it was later determined that Virginians from the Stonewall Brigade committed the crimes, Jackson had Starke arrested for insubordination but allowed him to remain in command.[75]

By Antietam, Starke's "approval rating" among his troops was no doubt at an all-time high. And it is very likely the general wanted to keep it that way. Leading two brigades—his own and Taliaferro's, 1,050 men total—Starke rode out in front of his men carrying the colors as he had at Manassas. Soon, the Rebels came under deadly fire from elements of the Iron Brigade. The now-thinned Confederate battle line made it to the Hagerstown Road, where it exchanged volleys with Gibbon's "Black Hats." Soon, the "Red Legged" 14th Brooklyn and green-clad 2nd U.S. Sharpshooters came to Gibbon's assistance. This phase of the morning action has been depicted numerous times in both period and modern artistic renditions, and photographer Alexander Gardner caught the bloody aftermath of the affair in his photograph of the Southern bodies, grotesquely stiff, lying

Confederates rallying along the Hagerstown Turnpike. *Antietam National Battlefield.*

Confederate dead along the Hagerstown Turnpike. *Library of Congress.*

along the Hagerstown Pike. In less than thirty minutes, Starke's Brigade lost almost 300 killed and wounded, while Taliaferro's Brigade lost 170 killed and wounded.[76]

Nine officers of the brigade were killed, including Starke. He never made it to the road but rather was hit almost simultaneously by three bullets that knocked him off his horse about 140 yards west of Hagerstown Pike. The brave general died within an hour, the first of six general officers (three Union and three Confederate) to be killed or mortally wounded in the battle.[77]

Union reinforcements and increased artillery fire finally drove the Rebels back across the road into the woods. Momentarily, there existed an opportunity for Hooker's battered ranks to make it to the Dunker Church. Incredibly, by 7:00 a.m., more than four thousand Rebs and Yanks were causalities. Much of Jackson's defense had dissolved to nothing as wounded and able-bodied stragglers made their way to the safety of the

West Woods. Jackson ordered Jubal Early's one-thousand-man brigade to move from the Nicodemus Heights area, where it supported Stuart's guns, to the West Woods in case it was needed to blunt Hooker's attack. It would replace Jackson's Division (led by Jones, Starke and Colonel Andrew Grigsby, in that order, during the past two hours of fighting), which was reduced to about three hundred effectives.[78]

With two divisions shattered, Jackson sought more reinforcements. Hood's Division, which included the brigade of Texans that bore his name, had been without a hot meal for several days. Accordingly, Jackson had given permission for Hood to put them in the rear behind the Dunker Church the previous evening. Now, just after 7:00 a.m. on the seventeenth, they were just getting started with cooking a hot breakfast when they were called up to reinforce the shattered Southern left flank. Now Hood's men were angry that their first hot meal in days had been interrupted, and they were ready for a fight. One Rebel officer wrote, "I have never seen a more disgusted bunch of boys and mad as hornets."[79]

What followed was one of the most legendary attacks of the war. The Texans, along with the rest of Hood's men, formed for battle in a field across the Hagerstown Pike just east of Dunker Church (this is in the

Sergeant Uriah P. Olin, Company B, 2nd Wisconsin Infantry. Killed at Antietam in or around the Cornfield. *Peter Dessauer Collection, Antietam National Battlefield.*

Brigadier General John Bell Hood. *Library of Congress.*

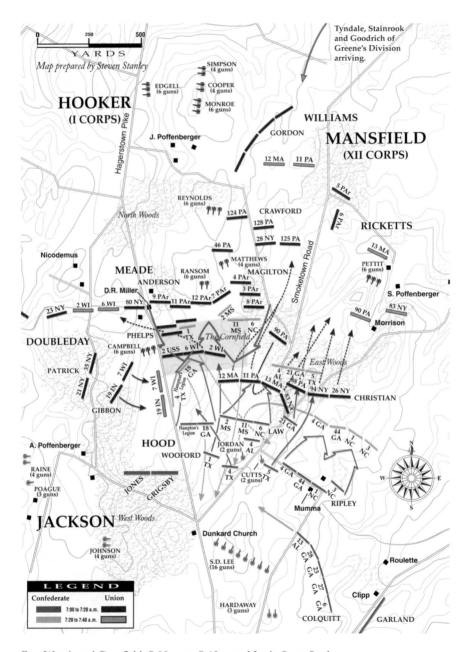

East Woods and Cornfield, 7:00 a.m.–7:40 a.m. *Map by Steven Stanley.*

locale where the Maryland State Monument stands today on the battlefield). By 7:20 a.m., Hood's two thousand men moved out, stepping over the dead, wounded and other debris of battle already incurred that morning. Hood's attack artillery, Battery B, 4th United States, worked feverishly pouring canister into the Texans and Georgians of the "Texas Brigade." Of all the Union batteries on the field that day, the men of Battery B suffered the most losses: forty men killed and wounded. For these regulars, the intensity of combat exceeded anything they had experienced up to then. Sergeant Joseph Herzog was shot through the lower bowels as he attempted to shift his gun to a new position. To the horror of his comrades, Herzog pulled out his pistol and ended his agony with a bullet to the temple.

The 1st Texas made the farthest incursion into the Cornfield sector. Trading shots with the Pennsylvania Reserves, and receiving damaging canister fire from Union guns, the Texans got the worst of it. The 1st Texas lost more than 82 percent of its men, the largest percentage loss for any unit North or South during the war.[80]

Another Union corps arrived on the north part of the battlefield as Hood's Division came up. This was the Twelfth Corps, under General Joseph F. Mansfield. Hooker sought the assistance of this command about 6:00 a.m. However, at that time, Mansfield and his men were more than one mile away and cooking their breakfast. Of all the Union corps at Antietam, this was probably the least experienced and the weakest numerically, with fewer than seventy-five hundred men. Some of its regiments were veterans of hard campaigning at places like Cedar Mountain and were greatly reduced in numbers; some units had as few as one hundred men in the ranks. Their commander, fifty-nine-year-old General Mansfield, had been an engineer officer with the inspector general's office. He had never led large bodies of troops in combat and took command of the Twelfth Corps just two days prior to the battle. Worse yet was the fact that about half of the corps' 1st Division was composed of green troops that had never seen combat. Although these men were brave, they lacked skills in basic military duties such as marching to the field and maneuvering when they arrived. At one point during the confusion of combat that morning, some of the soldiers fired into the backs of their own men.[81]

When the Twelfth Corps arrived on the field about 7:15 a.m., part of the command went to the aid of Hooker to repulse Hood. Mansfield personally led part of his first division—three veteran regiments, the 10th Maine, 28th New York and 46th Pennsylvania—into combat that day. Soon, they were exchanging fire with more Confederate reinforcements that had been sent to this sector.

Captain George Nye, Company K, 10th Maine. *Nicholas Picerno Collection.*

Captain Nehemia T. Furbush, Company I, 10th Maine. He was shot in the head and killed in the East Woods. His blood and brains splattered Captain George Nye, who was nearby. *Nicholas Picerno Collection.*

These were brigades from Major General D.H. Hill's Division, which was positioned about one mile to the south at Piper Farm. With pressure mounting on Jackson's part of the field, three brigades—Colquitt, Garland (now under McRae following the death of Garland at Fox's Gap three days before) and Ripley—were sent to the vicinity of the East Woods and Cornfield. The first to arrive were Ripley and Colquitt, twenty-seven hundred men strong. About thirty minutes behind them was Garland's seven-hundred-man brigade. The fighting here was particularly vicious. Captain George Nye, Company K, 10th Maine, wrote to his wife, "Captain Furbish was killed close to me, some of his blood and brains flew in my face." He turned to see who had been shot, only to see another officer fall nearby.[82]

General Mansfield attempted to win the confidence of the men in his new command by leading by example. He rode about that morning, sometimes to the dismay of his subordinate commanders, who felt he was doing what is known in modern parlance as "micromanaging." When the old general saw his troops firing into what he believed to be the ranks of friendly troops, he rode up to the skirmish line waving his sword and yelling for them to cease firing. When his troops pointed out that it really was Confederates at their front, it was too late. A Rebel volley mortally wounded his horse and him. Mansfield was brought back to the Line Farm, where he expired the next morning.[83]

The mortal wounding of Mansfield brought about a temporary crisis in command on the Union right. It was now past 8:00 a.m., and command of Twelfth Corps fell to Brigadier General Alpheus Williams. With the First Corps shattered, Hooker requested that Williams do the impossible and cover all parts of the field on the Union left. Accordingly, the Twelfth Corps was utilized in a piecemeal fashion. Goodrich's Brigade of Greene's Division was sent to support Gibbon along the

Major General J.K.F. Mansfield. *From* Battles and Leaders.

September 1887 reunion of the 10th Maine Infantry in the East Woods near where General Mansfield fell. *Nicholas Picerno Collection.*

Hagerstown Pike near Miller Farm, individual Twelfth Corps regiments remained scattered between the East Woods and the Hagerstown Pike and the 125th Pennsylvania, a green unit, made its way to the Dunker Church largely unsupported. The only intact component of the Twelfth Corps to seriously influence the tactical scenario on the Union right for the rest of that morning would be Greene's Division).[84]

While various parts of the Twelfth Corps floundered about on the field, the First Corps had run out of steam. About 9:00 a.m., Joe Hooker was carried to the rear with a painful wound to the ankle. After three hours of fighting, twenty-seven thousand men in blue and gray had suffered eighty-seven hundred casualties, mostly in killed and wounded. As Hooker was brought back to McClellan's headquarters at the Pry House for medical care, he saw Major General Edwin V. Sumner leading his Second Corps onto the field. On the Confederate side, more reinforcements were being brought up, and J.E.B. Stuart and his top gunner, Captain John Pelham, were gathering every piece of artillery they could find to concentrate against the next Yankee onslaught. Soon, they had more than twenty guns deployed on a piece of ground known as Hauser Ridge.[85]

6

West Woods and Dunker Church

They fell like grass before the mower.

One of the worst tactical debacles at Antietam occurred about 9:00 a.m. All was chaos and carnage in the Cornfield and East Woods as Jackson's veterans limped off the field, as individuals and in groups, back to the safety of the West Woods and beyond. Even though the attacks of the Union First and Twelfth Corps were spent, thousands more Union soldiers were marching into the fray.[86]

Among them was the Second Corps, under sixty-five-year-old Major General Edwin V. Sumner, the oldest general on the field and the oldest active corps commander in the war. He was also a cousin to the well-known abolitionist senator from Massachusetts, Charles Sumner. Cousin Charles was the leader of the Radical Republicans in the Senate and had the ignominious distinction in 1856 of being beaten with a cane on the senate floor by Congressman Preston Brooks of South Carolina.[87]

Edwin Sumner's military resume was superb, with more than forty years of military service. In the decades before the war, he served as a dragoon and cavalry commander. During the Mexican War, he earned acclaim as a cavalry commander under General Winfield Scott and received brevet promotions to lieutenant colonel and colonel. It was during this conflict that an enemy musket ball was said to have struck him in the forehead, causing no damage. This event is one possible source of his nickname, "Bull," short for "Bullhead." Another theory is that he was called "Bull" because of his booming voice. Besides fighting in Mexico, Sumner spent most of

Major General Edwin Sumner.
Library of Congress.

his prewar military career on the frontier leading the U.S. Cavalry against Indians. In 1855, he was promoted to colonel of the 1st U.S. Cavalry at Fort Leavenworth, Kansas. There, he took part in suppressing partisan forces during the "Bleeding Kansas" period.[88]

Sumner's command was the largest on the field that day: fifteen thousand strong.

When Sumner arrived on the field about 8:30 a.m., he had with him only part of his corps—the fifty-two-hundred-man division of Major General John Sedgwick. Connecticut-born Sedgwick saw service prior to the war against the Seminoles, in Mexico and on the Texas frontier. On the peninsula, he was wounded and recovered just in time for Antietam. Much beloved by his men, he suffered three wounds here and went on to greater fame at Fredericksburg and Gettysburg, only to meet death from a sharpshooter's bullet to the head on May 9, 1864, at Spotsylvania.[89]

Sedgwick's Division was one of the most experienced commands on the field that day. All but one regiment—the 59th New York—was combat tested, and experienced officers, many of them West Point graduates, could be found throughout the division. Most of Sedgwick's men, except for two regiments, carried rifled muskets. Two sharpshooter companies, armed with state-of-the-art breech-loading rifles, were attached to the division. The 1st Company, Massachusetts Sharpshooters, was attached to the 15th Massachusetts. They carried the Merrill rifle, a well-built, accurate weapon but with fragile paper cartridges. Attached to the 1st Minnesota was the 2nd Company, Minnesota Sharpshooters. They were issued the Sharps breech-loading rifle. These weapons could fire at a rate of seven to ten rounds per minute and were as accurate as the standard-issue muskets. However, unlike the muzzleloading musket, they could be fired from the prone position.[90]

French's and Richardson's Divisions were still marching some thirty to sixty minutes behind Sedgwick. Richardson had been kept at McClellan's headquarters as a reserve. When Sumner arrived on the field in the vicinity of the East Woods, he had to make a decision—and fast. A quick personal reconnaissance toward Hagerstown Road showed the Confederate left practically defenseless. Should he wait for the rest of the Second Corps to come up or move immediately to finish the job and maybe defeat Lee's army and end the war? Accordingly, the white-haired commander decided not to waste any further time. He would move into the West Woods and mop up Lee's left.

Sedgwick's Division was formed in a column of brigades. Each line had two ranks with an interval between the lines of about seventy-five yards. No skirmishers were deployed for this attack; the tight formation was designed to give the maximum shock value when it met an opponent. This was a very powerful and effective combat formation but could be a deadly one if caught in crossfire. Sumner personally led the division out of the East Woods and across open fields toward the Hagerstown Pike and the West Woods beyond.[91]

Sumner had no way of knowing that Lee was utilizing

Major General John Sedgwick. *Library of Congress.*

his interior line—at the Hagerstown Pike—to send more troops to bolster Jackson's shattered left flank. Two Confederate divisions—McLaws and Walker—numbering more than five thousand men moved "on a collision course with thunder today, for I have been dreaming that we were in the hardest battle yet." McLaws and his men rested in the early morning darkness not far from Lee's headquarters along the Shepherdstown Pike west of Sharpsburg. His command replaced Walker's as the army's reserve. Meanwhile, Walker was ordered to take his division and hold the Confederate right in the vicinity of the Rohrbach Bridge. Also, General Early moved his thousand-man reserve from Nicodemus Heights to the western edge of the West Woods. Further Confederate firepower was gained from a grouping of about thirty cannons collected by General J.E.B. Stuart and positioned just beyond the woods on Hauser Ridge, within easy range of the Union advance. Thus, the scene was set for a Union disaster as Sedgwick's Division moved forward in its tight formation.[92]

McLaws's men had marched much of the fairly warm night (sixty-five degrees) from Harpers Ferry, and many of the gray-clad troops were "still without provisions." One soldier, Private Leonard Taylor of the 32nd Virginia, had a hint of what was in store for the men that day. Just before breaking camp, he said, "Boys, we are going to catch thunder today, for I have been dreaming that we were in the hardest battle yet."[93]

Although not part of Sedgwick's Division, the 125th Pennsylvania, a Twelfth Corps unit, had advanced to Hagerstown Pike, opposite the Dunker Church, that morning. This fresh nine-month regiment from western Pennsylvania had been in service just over a month and carried more than seven hundred men into the battle. Mexican War veteran Jacob C. Higgins was the regimental commander. The core of the regiment was formed by a group of volunteers raised by a devout Scots-Irish Presbyterian named William W. Wallace. This group formed Company C and was dubbed the "Huntington Bible Company," since the people of Huntington, Pennsylvania, gave each volunteer a Bible. Wallace, now company commander, held frequent prayer meetings and adopted the motto "In God We Trust" for Company C. Soon, this became the motto for the entire regiment.

Earlier that day, the 125th had served as lead unit in the Twelfth Corps movement into the vicinity of East Woods. This put the green Pennsylvanians into combat for the first time as they exchanged fire with elements of the Texas Brigade. Soon, the 125th was forced back into the woods, where it continued to exchange fire with various Rebel commands. Following Mansfield's mortal wounding, the Pennsylvanians were ordered forward toward the intersection of Smoketown Road and Hagerstown Pike.

As the regiment reached this juncture, it came upon Monroe's Battery D, 1st Rhode Island, engaged in an artillery duel with Confederate guns west of the Hagerstown Pike. Instantly, the men of the 125th hit the dirt and lay prone as shot and shell whizzed overhead. This move was timed just right as a shell knocked second in command Lieutenant Colonel Jacob Szink off of his horse, seriously wounding him. Adding to the nervousness of the men was the horrific wounding of one of the cannoneers, as one of Monroe's men had a leg severed below the knee from an enemy solid shot. Meanwhile, as in all wars, humorous incidents occurred. In the midst of the artillery bombardment, a puppy belonging to the battery fled in fright and jumped down the blouse of Private Albert Robinson of Company G, 125th Pennsylvania.

Just before Sedgwick's arrival, the Pennsylvanians were ordered into the West Woods by an unknown officer, possibly from General Samuel Crawford's staff. The regiment moved swiftly into the woods, driving scattered Confederates before it. The 125th was in the woods for about thirty minutes. For most of that time, it was unsupported. It was the first to be hit by the Rebel juggernaut. To say that all was confusion is an understatement. It was a bloodbath. Private Stephen Aiken of Company D took a bullet to the face, which broke his jaw, and another to the neck; he lay on the field for three days, yet survived.[94]

Sergeant Edward L. Russ was shot through the abdomen. He recalled, "While lying wounded a Confederate ran up seemingly to bayonet and rob me, but picking up an ambrotype picture, he asked, 'Is that yours?' I replied 'yes, that is my dear wife.' He at once placed it in my hand, gazed at me for a moment, and hastily rejoined his comrades."

Soon, one of Sedgwick's regiments, the 34th New York of Gorman's Brigade, arrived to support the 125th. A heavy firefight ensued, and the green 125th withdrew from the woods, reforming east of Hagerstown Road. In about twenty minutes, they lost 229 men killed or wounded out of about 700 engaged. One of the most dramatic incidents in the regiment's history occurred at Antietam. During the withdrawal out of the woods and across Hagerstown Pike, Sergeant George Simpson, the regimental color-bearer, fell with a bullet to the brain. He fell on the flag and stained it with blood oozing from his right temple. Corporal Eugene Boblitz of Company H grabbed the colors and was soon felled with a leg wound that crippled him for life. Several other soldiers were shot trying to save the colors. Finally, Sergeant W.W. Greenland snatched up the bloodstained banner and passed it on to Captain William Wallace, who used it to rally the regiment. About

200 men formed in line, and about 60 gathered around the much-contested colors in protection. In the twenty-first century, there is often much debate over how we treat the flag. In the Civil War, there was none. Many soldiers were willing to give their lives for that flag.[95]

Meanwhile, the 34th New York was in the woods totally unsupported by artillery or infantry. Seeing that the Confederates were trying to flank them, the commander of the 34th, Colonel James A. Suiter, requested and received permission to fall back east of Hagerstown Pike. The 34th's short sojourn in the battle cost 33 killed, 111 wounded and 10 missing or captured. But the bloodletting had just begun.

With the retreat of the 34th New York, Sedgwick's left flank was now held by the 15th Massachusetts. This regiment had been mustered into service during the summer of 1861 and witnessed plenty of combat prior to Antietam. The 15th was present at the disastrous Battle of Ball's Bluff in the fall of 1861 and at all the major action on the peninsula from Fair Oaks to Malvern Hill. In August, the New Englanders had helped cover the Union retreat at Second Bull Run. Antietam proved to be the bloodiest day in the history of the 15th Massachusetts.[96]

After-action reports, postwar accounts and campaign studies often give the impression that units move neatly around battlefields like so many knights and pawns on a chess board. The reality is something different. The average "grunt," whether at Antietam, Iwo Jima or Fallujah, rarely knows much about what is occurring in combat except for in the few feet around him. All is mass confusion, and the main hope is to survive the immediate threat. The action in Antietam's West Woods was no exception.

Sergeant Jonathan P. Stowe, Company G, 15th Massachusetts, recalled the confusion, bullets, artillery shells and falling tree limbs. Charles Frazer, of Company C, wrote a vivid letter to his wife describing how the regiment's color guard was nearly wiped out and he was wounded three times. "The first one hit me in the arm but fortunately only left a [black and blue] mark. The next one hit me in the arm but it struck your likeness in my pocket and glanced off without injuring me. The next one hit me on the right hand." This last wound broke the bone in his thumb. George Fletcher of Company H was saved by a *Harper's Weekly* that he had received at mail call that morning. The newspaper was folded up and in his blouse pocket, stopping a bullet from penetrating his chest. Not all the Fletcher brothers were so fortunate that morning. Brother Samuel caught his brother James as he fell, shot through the head. Of the 62 men in Company H who went into the woods, only 9 walked out. The brutal twenty-minute ordeal of the

Veterans of the 15th Massachusetts at their monument dedication. *Antietam National Battlefield.*

15th Massachusetts cost that unit more than half its men. Out of 606 soldiers engaged, 75 were killed, 255 were wounded and, of those, forty-three later died of their wounds.[97]

As the rest of Gorman's Brigade moved through the woods and to its western border, it was stopped in its tracks by heavy Confederate fire to the front. Early's Confederates held a secure position in and around the Alfred Poffenberger farm buildings. Next came Dana's Brigade. They received heavy fire from Early's men to their front and from increasing Rebel fire to their left flank. To compound the confusion, the 59th New York, commanded by Lieutenant Colonel Lemuel Stetson, a cousin of the famous hat maker, collided with the left rear of the 15th Massachusetts. The green and frightened New Yorkers then began to fire through the Massachusetts unit in order to hit the enemy. This caused many Union casualties from "friendly fire." After much confusion, Sumner arrived and managed to get the New Yorkers to cease firing and fall back. The farthest Union advance was made by the 1st Minnesota on Sedgwick's right flank. They actually made it to the western edge of the woods, only to be stopped by the plunging fire of the Confederate guns on Hauser Ridge. The Minnesotans held steady enough to cover the retreat of part of Gorman's Brigade. One soldier in the regiment wrote to his sister from a field hospital the following day:

The Minnesota First was engaged about an hour when the order was given to fall back. I partially turned and was cautioning the men to move steadily when I was struck by a Minnie ball in my right thigh...When the ball struck me I fell and gathering myself up I made for the rear of the line of battle but our men fell back so far that I became exhausted and had to lie down. I hunted as secure a position as I could and in a short time the enemy were swarming around me as thick as bees. I talked to them good naturally and they were soon as social as any of our own people. When I found I could not escape I destroyed my gun and they would come along and pick it up and say "Where is the slide to this gun." Oh! Said I, Some of our boys threw it away—that is one of the tricks of war...The men and officers treated me very kindly while they were in possession of the field.[98]

Appropriately, the destruction of Sedgwick's Division has been dubbed the "West Woods Massacre." In about twenty minutes during the West Woods action, 373 Union soldiers were killed outright and 1,593 were wounded, many mortally. Approximately 244 were reported missing, and no doubt many of them were among the dead or dying.[99]

McLaws mounted a counterattack to follow up his success in the West Woods. Now it was time for the Rebels to get a taste of what they had dished out against Sedgwick. The brigade of General Paul Semmes diverged to the left, making it as far as the Miller Farm. In the process, Semmes's command was cut to pieces by Union artillery and musketry, several of his regiments losing more than half of their men. Elements of the Twelfth Corps, along with massed artillery around the Poffenberger Farm and on the edge of the East Woods and the rifled guns across the creek—in excess of forty

Lafayette McLaws. *Library of Congress.*

guns at various times—stopped McLaws's men in their tracks. Soon, these brave Confederates were retreating back to the safety of the West Woods, leaving the fields littered with the bodies of their comrades.[100]

Historians of the battle have been very critical of Sumner for his decision to move Sedgwick into the West Woods without waiting for the rest of his command to arrive on the field. To do so would have given Sumner about fifteen thousand men. However, this desire by historians for Sumner to wait assumes that the Confederates would also wait for this to happen. One of the characteristics of an effective commander is to exercise both caution and audacity at the appropriate times. Combat is a very fluid situation. Based on the information he had at the time, Sumner felt he could role up the Confederate left flank. After all, he and some of his staff had surveyed the field on horseback. Viewing the residual death and destruction from the combat of the previous three hours and seeing correctly that Confederate resistance on that part of the field had been crushed, Sumner decided to make his move, lest victory slip away. He had no way of knowing that Lee was sending McLaws and Walker to reinforce the Confederate left and that other Rebel units were deploying into this sector of the battlefield.

As the West Woods action was in progress, one of the least recognized yet most remarkable Union tactical achievements of the battle was rendered by the 2nd Division of the Twelfth Corps under sixty-one-year-old Brigadier General George Sears Greene. About 8:15 a.m., as General Mansfield was being carried off the field with his mortal wound, Greene's Division of around seventeen hundred men—less the brigade of Colonel Goodrich, which had been detached farther to the Union right—rushed from the East Woods, driving Ripley's and Colquitt's Rebels before them. The collapse of the Confederate line in this sector created a vacuum, which Greene was able to exploit. Soon, Greene's two brigades were in line opposite the burning Mumma Farm. There, he halted in the swale between the Mumma Farm building and the Dunker Church in order to regroup, replenish ammunition and wait for artillery support. The latter was provided by the arrival of Battery A, 1st Rhode Island Light Artillery, of Sedgwick's Division. This battery of six- to ten-pound Parrott rifles was commanded by Captain John A. Tompkins.[101]

Greene's Division advanced to the ridgeline between Dunker Church and the Mumma Farm buildings and was there at about 9:30 a.m., when Sumner entered the West Woods. Tompkin's Battery was already deployed on the ridge to Greene's left front. About 9:45 a.m., as McLaws advanced on Sedgwick's flank in the West Woods, three South Carolina regiments

Left: Private John Lawrence, Battery A, 1st Rhode Island Light Artillery. He was killed at Antietam at age twenty-one. *Bob Robertson Collection, Antietam National Battlefield.*

Below: The burning of Mumma Farm during the battle. *Library of Congress.*

of Kershaw's Brigade peeled off to the right and attacked Tompkins's guns. The Rhode Island artillery met them with canister at point-blank range, causing them to withdraw in confusion and leaving the ground covered with Confederate dead and wounded. Greene's men assisted Tompkins in the Confederate repulse; the whole affair lasted no more than fifteen minutes, and Kershaw lost about half the men who made the attack. During the fighting, Corporal Jacob Orth of the 28th Pennsylvania fought hand to hand with the color-bearer of the 7th South Carolina. Although wounded in the shoulder, he captured the Rebel flag

Brigadier General George S. Greene. *Library of Congress.*

in the process. After the war, Orth received the Medal of Honor for his act of bravery. The Yankees were appalled at the damage they had wrought. One soldier wrote, "The rebs were actually piled upon one another and those who were wounded beged [*sic*] for heaven's Sake not to murder them; we let them know that was not our business, to murder wounded men."[102]

Kershaw's attack was followed by another Confederate onslaught, this time from the North Carolinians and Virginians in three regiments of Colonel Van H. Manning's Brigade of Walker's Division. A member of the 48th North Carolina wrote, "We were all cut to pieces." Indeed, at a distance of about sixty yards, Manning's brave soldiers were only able to endure the deadly volleys of Greene's men and the canister of the Rhode Islanders for a matter of minutes before fleeing back to the shelter of the West Woods with the Yankees in pursuit. An Ohio soldier recalled, "They

Private Daniel Harrison Cox, Company G, 46th North Carolina Infantry, wounded and taken prisoner at Antietam. *Antietam National Battlefield.*

fell like grass before the mower." In this brief storm of death, Manning suffered 77 killed, 387 wounded and 41 missing, a total of 505 men cut down. The worst hit was the 30th Virginia. This was a unit composed of shopkeepers, clerks, skilled craftsmen and farmers from the Fredericksburg area. They went into the fight with 236 men and lost 172, killed, wounded and captured, 68 percent of the regiment.[103]

By about 10:30 a.m., Greene's Division was in possession of the Dunker Church and the section of the West Woods immediately behind it. Tompkins's Battery remained east of the pike in close support. In about two and a half hours of combat, the battery expended more than one thousand rounds of ammunition—a tremendous rate of fire for Civil War artillery. Tomkins withdrew about noon and was replaced briefly by Owen's Battery G, 1st Rhode Island, and a section of Joseph M. Knap's Pennsylvania Battery. Greene held the woods and church area for about two hours.

Two other Twelfth Corps units—the Purnell Legion (Maryland Infantry) and 13th New Jersey—arrived to support Greene. However, by 12:30 p.m., all the Union components of this incursion into the Confederate lines were weary from the morning's combat and seriously low on ammunition. Unsupported and threatened by increased Confederate pressure on his flanks, Greene withdrew back to the East Woods at about 12:30 p.m. Greene's unsupported movement and tenure in the West Woods is in some ways reminiscent of the legendary "Lost Battalion" of World War I fame. Indeed, it could be termed "Antietam's Lost Battalion." Greene's Division advanced farther and remained in

Dunker Church. *Library of Congress.*

action longer than any other Union division that day. In the process, it lost 552 men killed, wounded and missing, 31 percent of those engaged. Had it been reinforced with fresh units and resupplied with ammunition, the outcome of the Battle of Antietam may have been quite different.[104]

7

Bloody Lane

At about 9:30 a.m., French's fifty-seven-hundred-man division of the Second Corps arrived in the vicinity of the East Woods and veered south from there. D.H. Hill's twenty-six hundred Rebels were on the Sunken Road. We are not sure exactly why French did not move to support Sedgwick. Perhaps it was because that division was now hidden from view in the West Woods. Another possibility is that French saw Greene's Division and, thinking it to be Sedgwick's Division, maneuvered to fall in on its left. Whatever the case, for the next two and a half hours, French's troops attacked the Confederate center in what has been termed the "midday phase" of the Battle of Antietam. French, a native of Baltimore, had served out west before the war like many of his fellow officers.

Waiting to greet the bluecoats were about twenty-six hundred Rebels positioned in the sunken farm lane known locally as "Hog Trough Road." Their commander, Major General D.H. Hill, had earlier that morning sent two-thirds of his command north into the meat grinder of combat to support Jackson's men in the Cornfield and East Woods. Now the remnants of this force, primarily Garland and Colquitt's men, reinforced by Cobb's small brigade, held Hill's left flank. Toward the center of the line was the Alabama brigade of Brigadier General Robert E. Rodes. Hill's right flank was held by Brigadier General George B. Anderson's North Carolina brigade. These men were all veterans. Three days before the battle, he and his men had held Turners and Fox's Gap at South Mountain against overwhelming odds.[105]

Brigadier General William
French. *Library of Congress.*

Major General D.H. Hill. *From*
Lee's Lieutenants.

Ostensibly, the Federals would seem to have had the advantage in this attack since they outnumbered the Confederates more than two to one. However, here was another case of green troops being sent into battle and influencing the results. Of the ten regiments in French's command, four were brand new and two had seen very limited action. For example, the 1st Delaware had served since the beginning of the war, first as a three-month unit. However, its experience was relegated largely to garrison duty on the Virginia peninsula. The largely German 5th Maryland likewise saw little action, with the exception of some skirmishes. One entire brigade was composed of green regiments. Thus, about three thousand men out of French's total strength of fifty-seven hundred lacked combat experience. Also, the division had just been formed a few days before the battle while the army was on the march. Another factor that lessened the impact of French's assault was that it was made piecemeal by brigade, as opposed to using the force of his entire division.[106]

What followed was a bloody slugfest as each side stood its ground and blasted away at the other. Accounts indicate that in the first Confederate volley out on the road from Rodes's veterans, everyone in the front ranks of the Union assault fell, killed or wounded. The 1st Delaware was particularly hard hit. The regiment's color guard was wiped out, and every company commander was either killed or wounded. The regiment went into the fight with 650 men and lost 286 killed or wounded. The regimental commander's horse, Spot, was killed, and the men used it as a breastwork. To compound the situation, the 14th Connecticut, which had been mustered into service just weeks before and had never seen combat, panicked and fired a volley into the backs of the 1st Delaware. Soon, what had appeared to be an excellent natural fortification for the Confederates turned into a death trap, as French's men secured the high ground just north of the old road and poured volley after volley into the hapless Southern soldiers. By about 10:15 a.m., French's attacks had devolved into a stalemate, and D.H. Hill had been reinforced by about 3,300 men from General Richard H. Anderson's Division. French lost 1,750 men killed and wounded in his unsuccessful attack on the road. Rodes's command, in its immediate front, lost more than 200 killed and wounded.[107]

Soon, the rest of the Second Corps arrived on the field. This was the first division led by General Israel Richardson. Nicknamed "Greasy Dick" by his men, Richardson was one of the most aggressive commanders on the field that day. He led one of the most experienced Union commands in the battle. Most of his regiments were composed of seasoned combat veterans.

Major General Israel
Richardson. *Joseph Stahl
Collection.*

Among the most acclaimed of his brigades was the Irish Brigade, composed
of tough Irishmen of the 63rd, 69th and 88th New York and the New England
"Blue Bloods" of the 29th Massachusetts.

Richardson's Division battled the Rebels in the road for about an hour.
Finally, as so often happens in battles, a number of factors brought about
the collapse of the thin gray line on the Sunken Road. Hill's right, held by
the North Carolina Brigade of G.B. Anderson, began to crumble under
the pressure of the Irish Brigade and Caldwell's men. Meanwhile, Colonel
Francis Barlow led two small New York regiments into the lane, bisecting
the Confederate line. Finally, a confused order caused Rodes's men to filter
out of the lane, mistakenly believing the order had been given to pull back
to Piper Farm. Soon, the entire Confederate line was relinquishing the lane
and heading for the Piper farm buildings.[108]

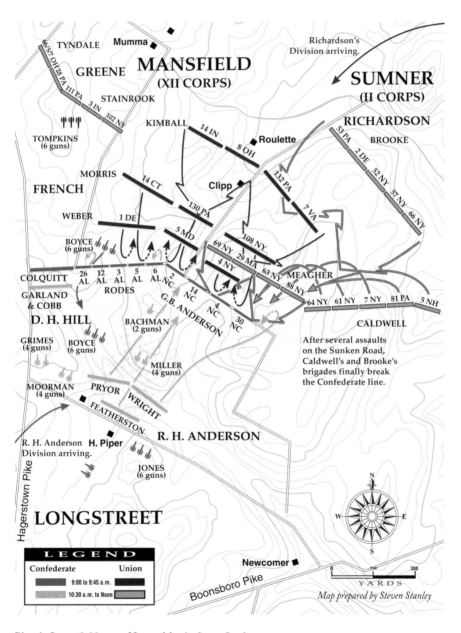

Bloody Lane, 9:00 a.m.–Noon. *Map by Steven Stanley.*

At this juncture, Longstreet and Hill were doing all they could by utilizing hands-on leadership to stop the Union advance. D.H. Hill picked up a musket and led around two hundred soldiers in a counterattack to keep the Yankees at bay. At one point, Rebel infantry helped man some of the cannons, and Longstreet and his staff operated one of the guns.

Longstreet sought out Cooke to lead a demi-brigade consisting of the 3rd Arkansas, the 27th North Carolina and the remnant of Cobb's Brigade—about 950 men in all—to attack French's right on the Mumma Farm. In most battles, a charge would be sounded by drums or bugles. In this case, a fiddler with the 3rd Arkansas led the way. The brave attack was repulsed with more than 50 percent casualties. Cooke did manage to make French change his line, and this and other action in the same sector possibly influenced Union thinking in regards to the strength and resiliency of the Confederate army.

Meanwhile, Ransom's Brigade launched an attack out of the West Woods, driving Greene's "Lost Battalion" back to the East Woods. General G.T. Anderson deployed his men behind a stone wall along the Hagerstown Pike to shore up Hill's and R.H. Anderson's troops, who were regrouping at Piper Farm.

Aggressive action requires an aggressive commander. Richardson was just the man for the job. He was seeking additional artillery and looking for reinforcements when he received a mortal wound from a Confederate artillery shell. One of his opposing commanders, Confederate brigadier general George B. Anderson, also received a mortal wound during the fight for Bloody Lane. This was a ball to the foot that became infected and killed him a number of weeks later.[109]

The struggle for the Sunken Road rivaled the body count on the north end of the field. Almost three thousand Yankees were killed or wounded trying to take the road, nearly 30 percent of those engaged. More than twenty-five hundred Confederates fell in their brave defense of Bloody Lane.[110]

8

Burnside Bridge and Beyond

As the Confederate center at Piper Farm came to a near collapse, the Ninth Corps was making progress at the Rohrbach Bridge. All morning, elements of this command had futilely attempted to find a way across the creek. A successful crossing would have easily destroyed Lee's weakened right flank. Since Lee had pulled Walker's Division off that sector in the morning, the area overlooking the bridge was held by about 450 Georgians from the brigade of Brigadier General Robert Toombs, D.R. Jones's Division.[111]

A brief artillery duel in this sector early that morning nullified any serious Confederate battery support for Toombs's men. Later, a poorly coordinated attack by Crook's Brigade succeeded in getting some of his regiments to move off course to a position upstream from the targeted bridge. The 11th Connecticut, detached from Harland's Brigade to act as skirmishers for Crook, got the worst of it. Elements of this unit made it to the bridge and into the creek before they were cut to pieces by enemy fire. Casualties included regimental commander Colonel Henry Kingsbury, who was mortally wounded, as well as 139 of his men, killed and wounded, many of them floundering in the now bloody creek. Many of the soldiers were shot to pieces but survived. Alonzo Maynard of Company I was hit by four bullets that broke four ribs and destroyed his right lung, leaving him bedridden for five years.[112]

Next, Nagle's Brigade of Sturgis's Division tried to make a quick dash to the bridge. With the Rebel sharpshooters less than ten yards away, Nagle's bluecoats suffered a withering fire upon their flank as they moved up a road parallel with the creek. About one-third of the men of the 2nd Maryland were felled, killed or wounded. The other regiments in the attack met a

Burnside Bridge. *Library of Congress.*

similar fate. Within minutes, the 6th New Hampshire lost 18 of its 150 men, while the 9th New Hampshire halted some distance to the rear and traded volleys with the Rebels on the opposite shore.

About 1:00 p.m., Cox ordered another attack, this time with two regiments from Ferrero's Brigade, which up to this time had not been engaged. These units, the 51st New York and the 51st Pennsylvania, totaled nearly eight hundred men. Supported by the fire of about eight guns, as well as skirmishers from the 21st Massachusetts, Ferrero's men rushed forward led by Colonel John F. Hartranft of the 51st Pennsylvania. Predictably, this assault was also halted by Confederate musketry. But these troops did not fall back. Rather, they made a stand behind stone and rail fencing adjacent to the bridge, trading volley for volley. Soon, they were joined by the 21st and 35th Massachusetts. Within minutes, the opposing fire subsided; Toombs's men were running out of ammunition. Lieutenant Colonel Robert B. Potter of the 51st New York decided that now was the time to rush the bridge.

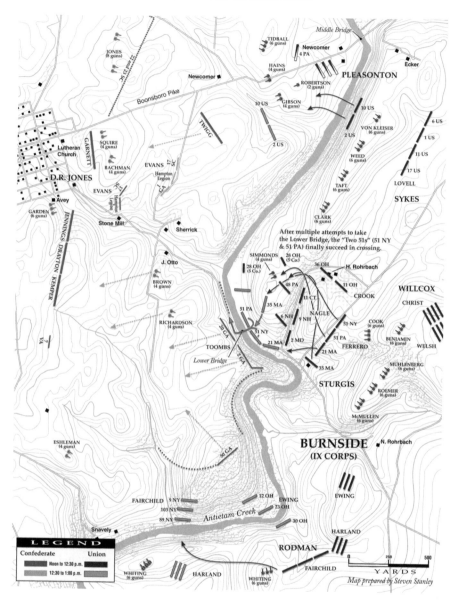

Burnside Bridge, Noon–1:00 p.m. *Map by Steven Stanley.*

Waving his sword, the gallant New Yorker led the charge as cheers went up from every Union command in the vicinity that could see it.[113]

By now, Brigadier General Isaac Peace Rodman's Division had crossed the chest-high creek, holding their weapons and cartridge boxes over their heads, downstream at Snavely's Ford. The threatened Confederate right flank responded with shrapnel rounds from artillery that one soldier exclaimed sounded like a "wild duck" flying over their heads. Running out of ammunition and facing Yankees on various fronts, the Confederates abandoned their positions. The Federals rounded up a few prisoners, particularly some sharpshooters who "were found in the trees, who could not make their escape." Soon, the rest of Cox's men were pouring across the bridge. As the men of the Ninth Corps ascended the hill previously held by the Georgians, and while others marched down the road to Sharpsburg, they were met with heavy canon fire from a number of Confederate batteries on the hills below Sharpsburg. This rain of artillery rounds kept the Union advance at bay. Burnside called a halt to the advance of the Ninth Corps. His troops rested, ate their chow and waited to replenish their ammunition.[114]

The fight for the bridge had cost the Union about 500 soldiers killed and wounded. In contrast, the defending Confederates suffered 120 casualties. But there would be more fighting and dying before the afternoon was over.

By about 3:00 p.m., more than eight thousand soldiers of the Ninth Corps were on the move in an irresistible line about one mile wide against Lee's crumbling right flank. To make matters worse for the Confederates, there were no more reserves available to Lee on the field, leaving him with fewer than three thousand infantry to defend his right. By 4:00 p.m., advance elements of the Union attack had cleared the ridges east of Sharpsburg of Confederate artillery and infantry and were entering the streets of the town. Simultaneously, but without any prior planning, the 4th U.S. Infantry of Sykes's Regular Division, Fifth Corps, advanced along the Boonsboro Pike supporting Cox's right flank.

The immediate Union threat to his flank had

Major General Ambrose Burnside. *Library of Congress.*

95

compelled Lee to go to a hill near his headquarters and scan the area to the south in hopes of seeing the arrival of A.P. Hill's Division from Harpers Ferry. A short time before the Union advance, at approximately 2:30 p.m., A.P. Hill—astride his iron gray mount, Champ, and accompanied by his staff—reported to the anxious Lee that his division was just an hour behind.

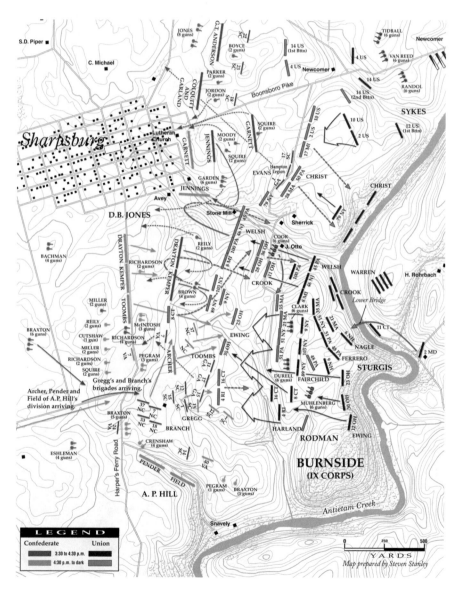

Lower Field, 3:30 p.m.–Dark. *Map by Steven Stanley.*

Immediately, plans were initiated to deploy Hill's thirty-two hundred men, now weary from the seventeen-mile forced march from Harpers Ferry

While waiting for Hill's men to arrive, Lee and his staff frantically scoured the area for additional men and guns. Here and there, groups of stragglers were pressed into service, augmenting the thin ranks of Evan's Brigade. A number of guns were collected from various batteries to stem the Yankee tide, including twelve additional cannons with caissons full of ammunition brought forth by Colonel Stephen D. Lee.

Between 3:30 and 4:00 p.m., just as it seemed that the Federals would crush the Confederate right flank, Hill's Division began arriving on the field. Attrition had taken its toll on the march that hot day, but in the lead was Brigadier General Maxcy Gregg's thousand-man brigade. Additional brigades would arrive not far behind in piecemeal fashion, but Gregg's one thousand South Carolinians, more than any other Confederates in this phase of the battle, would turn the tide.[115]

As Gregg's lines maneuvered onto the field, they were soon on the left flank of Rodman's Division, poised to strike. To compound this problem for the Yankees, the flank was held by the 16th Connecticut, one of the many green regiments on the field that day in the Army of the Potomac. When the Rebels struck, the young recruits from the Nutmeg State never had a chance. Soon, the 16th Connecticut was retreating in panic. Students of the

Major General A.P. Hill.
From Battles and Leaders.

battle still pursue the question of whether any of Hill's men, deliberately or inadvertently, deceived the Yankees by wearing captured Union uniforms from the vast stores at Harpers Ferry. While this story could be chalked up to postwar veterans' tall tales, I have found at least one reference to this, written by a soldier in the 16th Connecticut just three days after the battle.

Sergeant Jacob C. Bauer, Company C of the 16th, wrote home to his wife in a letter dated September 20: "We lost most of our men in a large cornfield where the rebels flanked us, they wore our clothes, flouted our flag, and told us not to fire on our own men. This put us in utter confusion."[116]

From here, the fighting devolved into confusion, especially for the Yankees. The 16th Connecticut, in its hasty withdrawal, ran right into the 4th Rhode Island, disrupting the lines of the regiment that was coming to support it. The Rhode Island ranks were further disrupted when a deadly volley from Gregg's troops hit them head on at short range. Shortly, like their New England neighbors in the 16th Connecticut, the Rhode Islanders were fleeing the field in confusion.

Soon, more of Hill's Rebels were attacking the Ninth Corps' advance. Brigadier General Lawrence O'Brien Branch's North Carolinians stopped Fairchild's Brigade, while Greggs's troops circled behind the isolated bluecoats. Seeing his position as untenable, Fairchild withdrew back toward

Attack of the 9th New York Infantry. *Antietam National Battlefield.*

Antietam Creek. As the rest of Hill's Division came onto the field, they were reinforced by the reformed commands of D.R. Jones. But by now Greggs's and Branch's Carolinians had hurled the Yankees back toward the creek.[117]

By 6:00 p.m., the fighting had died down to sporadic musketry and artillery fire. The Ninth Corps pulled back to the high ground overlooking the bridge, and the units on Lee's right held their positions on the hills east and south of Sharpsburg. The final phase of the fighting had been short and bloody. While the losses on both sides cannot compare with the carnage in the Cornfield, West Woods and Bloody Lane, they were still heavy for the duration of the combat and numbers engaged. The Ninth Corps suffered 2,249 casualties; of these, more than 400 were killed outright on the battlefield. The Confederates lost more than 1,000 men killed, wounded and missing holding the right flank that afternoon. This includes more than 140 killed in action, 66 of them in Hill's Division. During this final phase of combat, two more generals were killed: Rodman was mortally wounded while leading his troops, and Confederate Brigadier General Lawrence O'Brien Branch was killed instantly by a bullet to the head toward the end of the battle as he surveyed the bloody landscape with his binoculars. More than 23,000 men, Americans all, became casualties that day. The Battle of Antietam was over.[118]

9

One Vast Hospital

The only thing worse than a battle lost is a battle won.

This utterance, attributed to the Duke of Wellington following his defeat of Napoleon at Waterloo, could be said for any Civil War battle, including Antietam.

The morning of September 18, 1862, revealed the bloody yield of the previous day's battle. Twelve hours of brutal combat rendered scenes that were never forgotten. Nearly four thousand dead bodies were scattered over a three-mile front. Otho Nesbitt of Clear Spring, Maryland, kept a detailed diary of the period. He visited the area on September 18 and 19 and wrote that "the whole country around about is a hospital. Houses and barns full...I saw a man with a hole in his belly about as big as a hat and about a quart of dark—looking maggots working away."[119]

Colonel David Hunter Strother of McClellan's staff rode across the north end of the battlefield on the eighteenth and observed that the bodies of dead Confederates were "already far advanced in putrification, hideously swollen, and many of them black as soot."[120]

Hardened veterans were amazed at the carnage. Private Edward Burrus of the 21st Mississippi wrote to his parents:

> *I had the opportunity of going over the battlefield—in fact we were immediately on one of the very bloodiest parts of it. It is no figure of speech, metaphor or anything but a simple fact to say that there were frequently places where for 50 or 60 yards you could step from one dead Yank to*

another and walk all over the ground without once touching it with your foot. On one little knoll about 25 or 30 yds. square I myself counted 189 dead Yankees and they were no thicker there than in many other places.[121]

The 145th Pennsylvania had arrived on the field too late for the battle, but they drew the dubious assignment of burial detail. One soldier left a vivid account of the macabre scenes of Antietam's aftermath in a letter to his local newspaper:

Before me is a stubble field covered with dead bodies of men and horse. Behind that fence which is full of bullets, the rebels lie very thick—from the manner in which they lie you can see how the line of battle was formed... The trees are splintered and torn; houses are riddled, the ground is covered [with] crackers and canteens and haversacks and knapsacks that fell from, or were thrown away by the wounded or dying there are found thousands on thousands of bullet, grape, cannon balls, shells, muskets, swords, etc. etc.

He went on to write:

But I can only see and think about those dead bodies. Most of them look as black as the darkest negroes; they are greatly swollen and fearfully distorted some scarcely looking like human beings. Black blood and putrid matter are

Burial of the dead at Sunken Road. *Antietam National Battlefield.*

still oozing from the wounds in their heads, breasts and sides. They fell in every conceivable manner, and some lie as they fell, and others try to twist themselves into a more comfortable position. I will not speak of those eyes open as if staring at you, of the lips parted as if to address you, of the hair clotted with blood, of the hands pressing the wound or folded as if in prayer, for I am sick of the sight, which still haunts me and causes a chill to pass over my frame.[122]

The story was the same everywhere one turned. Scenes of death dominated the landscape. In Sharpsburg, dead bodies, mostly Confederates, were found in gardens, alleys and parlors. One local story tells of the Grice family returning to their home and being shocked to find three dead Confederates lying inside and two more in the yard.[123]

Besides the dead soldiers, there were also large numbers of dead horses and other animals. The army paid local farmers to collect and burn the carcasses. Most of these were destroyed where they had fallen. Near the Hagerstown Pike, Otho Nesbitt saw a "white bull or steer lying on his back all swelled up and 2 sheep nearby all swelled up and ready to burst." In a letter to his wife, Captain David Been of Company H, 14th Indiana, wrote that "hundreds of dead horses strew the fields in every direction." In Sharpsburg, dead horses were seen lying in the streets for days.[124]

John P. Smith, a boy at the time and later the town historian, recalled that "the stench arising from the battlefield was intolerable." Another citizen said "the stench was terrible. We had to close doors and windows to shut out the nauseating odor of decaying corpses." The stench was noticeable for miles away. Soldiers on the burial details often drank whiskey to kill the smell. Samuel Fletcher of the 15th Massachusetts had the misfortune to be on a burial party. He recalled the hot weather and that "the bodies were getting soft and it was very unpleasant…I tasted the odor for several days."[125]

After a battle, it was important to dispose of the bodies as soon as possible. Typhoid, cholera and other diseases could be spread by contact with dead bodies. The bloated corpses attracted disease-spreading flies. Union burial details began their work on September 19. At first, the focus was on the Union dead. The next day, burial details started on the Confederates. The whole process took about four days. However, farmers continued finding bodies under ledges and bushes for some time afterward. Many of the Antietam dead, particularly the Confederates, were buried in shallow graves, later to be rooted up by hogs. At some points on the field, the Confederates ended up in mass burial trenches, such as one on the Roulette Farm, where seven hundred men were buried.[126]

For some of the locals, the battle was a financial boon. The Dunker Church was used as an embalming station. There, this relatively new science was being practiced by contractors for those families who could afford it. Local farmers made extra money hauling coffins with embalmed Union soldiers from the church to the railroad station in nearby Hagerstown.[127]

About nineteen thousand men were wounded in the battle. Their care posed a logistical challenge that encompassed an area of more than forty miles and parts of three states. Practically every house, church, barn and shed in and around Sharpsburg, more than 120 structures, was used as some sort of hospital. But beyond that, the wounded were taken to hospitals in nearby villages such as Keedysville and Boonsboro. Frederick and Hagerstown, Maryland, became major hospital sites, and about four hundred wounded Union soldiers were sent north by rail to Chambersburg, Pennsylvania. The Confederates set up hospitals in Shepherdstown, Martinsburg and Winchester, Virginia. A Hagerstown newspaper referred to the area as "one vast hospital."[128]

By the time of the Vietnam War and up until our present conflicts in the Middle East, medical evacuation of the wounded has generally been swift. The use of motor vehicles or aircraft, particularly the helicopter, allows for medevacs, often in thirty minutes or less. During the Civil War, wounded soldiers usually stayed on the field much longer. Antietam was no exception. Accounts tell of soldiers lying out on the battlefield for two or three days.[129]

However, a revolution in combat medical care was instituted just a few weeks prior to Antietam to alleviate this. Dr. Jonathan Letterman, chief medical officer of the Army of the Potomac, organized an ambulance corps that moved to the front to evacuate the wounded and established field hospitals and a procedure to prioritize causalities by the severity of their wounds. This system is what emergency medical teams today know as triage.[130]

Viewing the operations of a Civil War field hospital was an experience never forgotten by those who had the dubious opportunity to do so. John P. Smith was a boy at the time of the battle. He vividly recalled the gore present at a Confederate hospital on the Harry Reel farm:

I saw a number of wounded and dead Confederates brought into the yard. Some were having limbs amputated, others horribly mangled, were dying. One man in particular I shall never forget. His entire abdomen had been torn and mangled by a piece of exploded shell. He uttered piercing and heart rendering cries, and besought those who stood by for God's sake to kill him

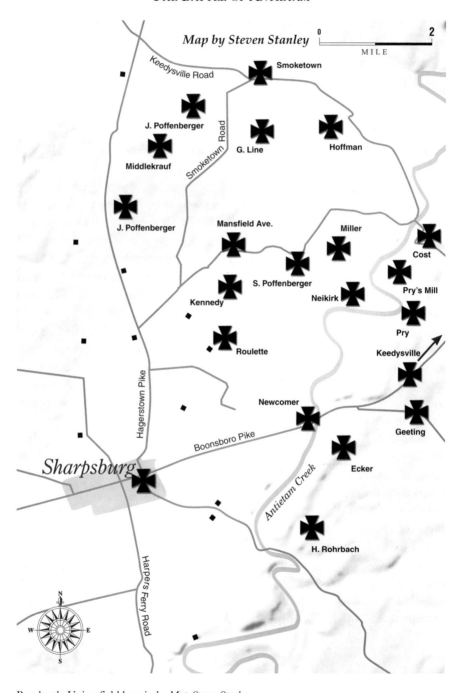

Post-battle Union field hospitals. *Map Steven Stanley.*

and thus end his sufferings. Death however came to his relief in a short time and he was hastily buried in a shallow grave.

One can only speculate what effect such scenes had on the many local children who witnessed them.[131]

The perceived glory of war, portrayed in so many battle scenes rendered by artists, was torn away by the realities manifested by ghastly, disfiguring wounds. A trooper in the 3rd Pennsylvania Cavalry survived a cannonball that grazed his cheek, tearing it completely off and depositing it onto a nearby comrade. Private William Kidd of the 16th Mississippi received what was believed to be a canister wound through the face, carrying away the muscles of both cheeks, his nose and his right eye. This caused his upper jaw to fall over his lower jaw and chin, leaving his palate and throat exposed. Although his Confederate surgeon deemed his case hopeless, when he fell into the hands of Union surgeons, he was soon up and about walking the streets of Sharpsburg.[132]

Many a wounded soldier lay out on the field for several days. Private Samuel Dilburn of the 6th Alabama was wounded in the side and left out on the

Field medical care. *Antietam National Battlefield.*

Clara Barton. *Library of Congress.*

field for dead. Maggots soon invaded his wound. They only eat dead flesh, so he was saved from contracting gangrene. Dilburn was eventually found among the dead and taken to an aid station. Upon his recovery, he was imprisoned at Fort Delaware and exchanged in 1864. Despite his bad wound at Sharpsburg, the young Alabamian survived the war.[133]

Much has been written about the work of Clara Barton, the "Angel of the Battlefield" and, later, founder of the American Red Cross. While her endeavors were commendable, local citizens did their part as "angels" also. Among them was Mrs. Angela K. Davis of Funkstown, a village on the National Road about eight miles away. She and her husband directed both Union and Confederate sympathizers in their town to prepare food to take to the wounded. In her very vivid *Reminiscences*, she wrote, "We sat up most of the night, killing and cooking chickens etc. and the next morning our dining room, kitchen and wash house were all filled with jars or crocks of mashed potatoes, fried ham, chicken and beef sandwiches." Davis recalled that "we distributed the sandwiches as best we could (which seemed like a drop in the bucket)."[134]

Ladies' aid societies, volunteer groups formed in communities throughout the North, also did their part. For example, in the little town of Mercersburg, Pennsylvania, about forty miles to the northwest of Sharpsburg, the ladies packed up a number of boxes destined for military hospitals in the region. These included assorted foodstuffs such as jelly, canned fruit, dried fruit, pickles, catsup and bottles of wine. One box specifically directed to Sharpsburg contained lint, bandages, rags and one bottle of wine.

Despite food shortages in the immediate area, the historian of the 13th Massachusetts recalled:

We cannot forebear mentioning the generosity shown by the people of the surrounding towns, who came on to the field the day following the battle, with food and supplies from their homes, not only for the wounded, but for the men who had escaped that misfortune. The people from Middletown, Sharpsburg, Hagerstown, and even Hancock, forty miles away, were inquiring for the Thirteenth Massachusetts Regiment. Hancock sent a four-horse team loaded with food and delicacies for the wounded. The greatest pleasure of all was to see the faces of our friends of the previous winter, and to feel that our service among them had left no unpleasant impression.

The 13th Massachusetts had been stationed in Hancock the year before.[135]

Even though the armies left Sharpsburg, some of the hospitals existed well into the following year. For some, the scars of the event could not be visibly measured. Because of looting by Union soldiers after the battle, leaving the family destitute, Mrs. Jacob Houser "was taken suddenly ill from fright and could not be moved for weeks after the battle."[136]

All of the wagons, artillery with limbers and caissons and the thousands of men and horses put a great strain on roadways, as well as surrounding pastures. For example, the Hagerstown Pike was built about 1856, so it was a relatively new highway at the time of the battle. It was nearly ruined by the armies going back and forth over it. However, the pike company received damage compensation from the Federal government. Others were not so fortunate.[137]

Since forage was of the greatest weight, as much of it as possible would be "requisitioned from the local populous." An editorial in the *Hagerstown Herald and Torchlight* of September 24, 1862, reported that

the region of the county between Sharpsburg and Boonsboro has been eaten out of food of every description. The two armies…have swept over it and devoured everything within reach. At Sharpsburg, we understand that the Rebels sacked the town, and when they left many of the citizens had not a morsel to eat…The amount of personal property—horses, cattle, hogs, sheep, corn, hay, and other provender—which was taken from the farmers, was enormous, the whole lower portion of our county has been stripped of every description of subsistence, and what our people in that section of the county will do to obtain food for man and beasts during the approaching winter, God alone knows.[138]

The presence of thousands of soldiers would obviously have an impact on the ecology of the area—a fact often overlooked by modern visitors to Civil

War battlefields with their neatly mowed lawns and well-maintained tour roads. Also, it is often forgotten that besides thousands of soldiers, the armies needed animals to pull their equipment. On October 1, 1862, the Army of the Potomac had 22,493 horses and 10,392 mules. The number for the Confederates can only be estimated. Lee stated that "we are deficient in transport." In fact, at Antietam the average Confederate artillery battery had 4 horse teams. In many cases, wagons were being used in lieu of caissons. A rough estimate would be about 16,000 horses and mules on the Confederate side.[139]

Like their human counterparts, horses in the Civil War and in the Maryland Campaign also faced the problem of disease. One problem that plagued the horses of both armies since the beginning of the Maryland Campaign was known as "greasy heel"—a form of eczema. An oily secretion oozes from lesions on the horse's heel and pastern area, drying and becoming crusty. Swelling of the legs and lameness can result. The condition may be caused by standing in dirty stables, constant contact with dung and urine or working in deep mud.

The "greasy heel" epidemic started in the Army of the Potomac and manifested within a few days of marching from Washington during the first week of September. Union cavalry mounts subsisted on green cornstalks until September 20, a factor many thought had much to do with the epidemic.

Colonel Rufus Ingalls, McClellan's chief quartermaster, reported at the end of the campaign:

> *The artillery and cavalry required large numbers* [of horses] *to cover losses sustained in battle, on the march, and by disease. Both of these arms were deficient when they left Washington. A most violent and destructive disease made its appearance at this time, which put nearly 4,000 animals out of service.*

Equine diseases also affected the Confederates. By late October 1862, the cavalry of General Fitzhugh Lee's brigade had fewer than one thousand mounts because of "greasy heel," and some of his regiments could mount only one hundred men or fewer. Many artillery batteries in the Army of Northern Virginia were reduced from six- to four-horse teams to meet the crisis. Also, a hospital was established at Culpeper Court House, Virginia, where many of the horses were put in quarantine.[140]

The stench of nearly fifty thousand horses and mules was not only an inconvenience, but it was a tremendous health hazard as well. Each horse or mule produced an average of thirteen and a half pounds of manure and two gallons of urine per day. This, along with the waste of thousands of soldiers combined with the thousands of dead and wounded, threatened the local water supply and attracted disease-carrying insects, particularly flies.[141]

Disease, not bullets, was the major killer during the war. Incredibly, the rate of attrition in a Civil War regiment sometimes exceeded that of a bomber command in World War II. As medical historian Paul Steiner pointed out in his *Disease in the Civil War: Natural Biological Warfare in 1861–1865*, "The Civil War provided the last opportunity in the pre-microbiological era for the major pathogenic microbes to exhibit their maximum effects without effective deterrence." Chronic diarrhea and dysentery, malaria, typhoid fever and cholera were diseases common to both soldier and civilian prior to the twentieth century. According to Steiner, "Healthy, latent, or mildly ill carriers of the causative agents existed in every sizable group of Americans." Accordingly, if the Battle of Antietam were fought today, there would be much less of a public health threat from its aftermath. Many of the diseases mentioned above are no longer prevalent in the industrialized world, and it is only those diseases that are common before a disaster that are likely to be a threat after a disaster.[142]

The opposing armies would have brought much sickness with them during that fatal week of September 17, 1862, exposing the civilian population simply by their presence. The large amounts of both human and animal waste further enhanced the possibility for sickness.[143]

No definitive study has been done on disease among the civilian population as a result of the Battle of Antietam—or for that matter any other Civil War battle. However, the conditions were ripe for sickness, and anecdotal evidence suggests that illness was a major problem in the civilian population as a result of the presence of the armies and the battle. In a letter written nearly three months after the Battle of Antietam by Jacob Miller, a local farmer and prominent civic leader, he tells of the sickness and death around him:

> *Your Unkle* [sic] *Daniel Miller is no more…He was not well when he left home the day before the big battle…He came to town several times. After he got back he was taken with a diarear* [sic] *which was a very common complaint with the troops and citizens. Both armies were afflicted with the disease, however. Daniel took sick on Monday or Tuesday and continued getting worse with sick vomiting spells.*[144]

Miller's letter continues with a description of neighbors and friends that were afflicted by or had succumbed to sickness:

Mrs. Adam Michael is no more she took her flite [sic] *this day a weak* [sic].
Her oldest daughter had just gon [sic] *before her about eight or ten days…*
Hellen and Janet had a severe attack of tayfoy fevour [typhoid fever]
but are both getting better…Jacob and Annmarys children nearly all…had
Scarlet fevour [sic] *but are all geting* [sic] *well—Henry Mummas wife*
is no more, she departed this life about two weaks [sic] *since. She had the*
same fevour. Nearly all or quite all of john Smith family wore down but are
getting better. Many other citizens and hundreds of soldiers have been taken
with the same, and many died.[145]

The Michael family mentioned in Miller's letter were particularly
hard hit. Adam Michael lost not only his wife but also, as noted above,
the "oldest daughter," Elizabeth. In addition, Michael's son Caleb and
youngest daughter, Catherine, got sick but recovered. Another son,
Samuel, wrote a letter to his brother describing the tragedy and laying
the blame directly on the presence of a Union hospital established in
their house:

The hospital was continued in our parlor for several weeks. I do not know
how many has [sic] *died in it. They have left it now. It looks like a hog*
pen…the disease of the hospital has affected three of our family…Mother
died with this disease on the 25th *day of November. Was buried today by*
Mr. Adams and Shufford. We could not have no funeral for neither of them
had no place to preach. Mother complained but a short time was taken with
three very severe hemorrhages of the bowels—took place about 12 o'clock
at night, the first one. She died the next day 10 minutes before two. She was
a beautiful corpse.[146]

Death was ever present in the nineteenth century, particularly for children.
One month after the bloodbath on their farm, the Roulettes lost their
youngest daughter, Carrie May. This twenty-month-old child was described
as a "charming little girl," just beginning to talk. Whether at the hands of
the carnage of war or just the normalcy of disease in this period, Carrie
succumbed to typhoid fever.[147]

The town of Sharpsburg suffered great property damage during the
battle. Eyewitness accounts by soldiers confirm that "few were the houses
that had not been pierced by solid shot or shell." About three years after the
battle, it was noted that "on the side of the town fronting the Federal line of
battle every house bears its marks; indeed I do not know that any altogether

escaped." One civilian observed that some barns were "burnt," along with "4 or 5 small houses, and stables in Sharpsburg."[148]

About one hundred people hid in the cellar of Mr. John Kretzer on Main Street, among them a mother with a three-day-old child. A shell exploded just outside the cellar wall, causing panic among the people. A piece of shell struck the door of the Miller home in Sharpsburg and cut a piece out of the sill. Miss Savilla Miller was standing in the doorway at the time but escaped uninjured. Jacob McGraw had sought safety in the Kretzer cellar with scores of other citizens. In midafternoon, he ventured outside and down the street several blocks. He was standing outside his brother's hotel when a shell struck the brickwork above his head, showering him with fragments. McGraw immediately rushed back to the safety of the cellar.[149]

No evidence exists to support any claims of citizens being killed by artillery or small arms fire, although there have been unsubstantiated references to the death of a little girl from the bombardments. There is, however, abundant evidence that people got themselves blown up after the battle by tampering with unexploded artillery projectiles. One of them, John Keplinger, had cleared and "broke" about ninety-nine shells from fields around Bloody Lane. He was not so fortunate with number one hundred, which exploded and "tore him up so badly that he died from it."[150]

Similar damage occurred on every farm. Rail fences also took much abuse from artillery and small arms fire. Many were torn down to facilitate the movement of advancing troops, and later the rails were used as firewood by the armies.

The farms on the battlefield suffered the worst damage, probably more from plundering and vandalism than from combat.

In his damage claim to the Federal government, Henry Piper claimed $25 for both the house and barn. However, he claimed more than $2,000 in other damages. Ironically, most of the latter was attributable to Federal troops during their post-battle foraging. The 3rd and 4th Pennsylvania Cavalry and the 8th New York Cavalry were camped on the Piper property after the battle. Union infantry was also camped in the area. Household property was damaged or stolen, and all the livestock and harvested crops were taken.

Claim records indicate what livestock the Pipers lost: one roan mare, eight milk cows, two steers, fourteen other cattle, forty hogs, eighteen sheep, two hundred chickens, fifteen geese and twenty-four turkeys. Crops and foodstuffs taken or damaged included one hundred bushels of Irish potatoes, thirty bushels of sweet potatoes, two hundred bushels of apples, two hundred bushels of wheat, eight hundred pounds of bacon, three thousand pounds of lard and twenty acres of corn.[151]

Samuel Mumma suffered property damage amounting to about $10,000. on his farm. This included thirty-five tons of hay and several hundred bushels of wheat, corn and rye taken. Most of this damage was caused by Federal troops. Sadly, Mr. Mumma never got completely reimbursed for the losses; the government blamed most of them on the Confederates. The Joseph Sherrick House suffered $8 in damage from an artillery shell and $1,351 in damage from occupying Federal troops.

Of the hundreds of local citizens who suffered property damage during the battle and occupation of the two armies, the Mummas lost the most. On the morning of the seventeenth, the place was burned. It was the only private structure deliberately destroyed during the battle. Throughout the battle, the farm was the center of activity, either of combat or staging for combat. At various times during the battle, the farm was the target of Southern artillery.

The Mumma family moved into the Sherrick House on the south end of the battlefield until their place was rebuilt. They moved back in June 1863, just in time to see more Confederates marching by on their way to Pennsylvania.[152]

Another impact of the battle was the dislocation of civilians. Besides seeking refuge in local cellars, many fled to neighboring communities and farms. Some sought shelter along the banks of the Potomac at the Killingsburg Caves and other sites. Bud Shackleford was eighteen at the time. The day before the battle, he went to Snyder's Landing on the Maryland side of the river. There he saw about two hundred children staying at a farmhouse. The problem of feeding them was resolved when someone got two barrels of flour from a nearby warehouse. Soon, the children were all eating shortcakes.[153]

The great toll in life and limb from the battle was horrendous. For the Union, 2,108 men were killed outright. Another 9,540 were wounded, and many of them would die within days, weeks or months from their wounds. Approximately 753 were listed as missing. Some of them were no doubt taken prisoner or were killed and their bodies found later. The Confederates lost 1,540 killed, 7,752 wounded and 1,018 missing, for a total of 10,316. The Confederates may have underestimated their casualties and not counted so-called walking wounded—those men who perhaps suffered minor wounds. With this in mind, the toll at the battle was probably more than 23,000. Thus, the Battle of Antietam was the bloodiest one-day battle in American history. For many, soldier and civilian both, its impact would last a lifetime.[154]

As mentioned earlier, a lasting positive influence that came out of the battle was the implementation of a field medical system that was the precursor of modern first aid. Credit for this goes to the organizational genius of Dr. Jonathan Letterman, medical director of the Army of the Potomac.

With McClellan's complete support, Letterman reorganized the ambulance corps in the summer of 1862. Letterman also worked to improve the medical supply system and developed methods to prioritize the battlefield care of the wounded. The latter system we know today as triage. Letterman was able to implement many of his programs at Antietam. His system was eventually adopted by all the armies of the world.[155]

10

Henceforward and Forever Free

On September 19, McClellan was prepared to renew the battle. However, he soon found out that there were no Confederates opposing him in the fields and hills around Sharpsburg.[156]

Lee had defiantly held his Army of Northern Virginia in position throughout September 18. Late that night, he began to withdraw his shattered force across the Potomac back to Virginia via Boteler's Ford (also known as Blackford's, Packhorse or Shepherdstown Ford), about a mile and a half downstream from Shepherdstown. By dawn on September 19, Lee could confidently report that "the army was accordingly withdrawn to the south side of the Potomac without loss or molestation." Most of the Confederates were across the river, except for an artillery battery and some wounded men from Longstreet's command. The last action on Maryland soil in the Maryland campaign occurred about 9:00 a.m. that day when two companies of the 14th South Carolina repulsed and dispersed a Union cavalry detachment in a cornfield not far from the ford.[157]

By this time, McClellan concluded that Lee had given him the slip. Accordingly, McClellan directed a cautious pursuit toward the river. About 10:30 a.m. on the nineteenth, Union cavalry, led by General Alfred Pleasonton, was trading shots with elements of Lee's rearguard, the cavalry brigade of General Fitzhugh Lee, as it crossed at Boteler's Ford.

Heavy casualties had severely damaged the infrastructure of the Army of the Potomac. For McClellan, a full-blown pursuit of Lee was deemed out of the question. However, he did take steps to constrict Lee's movements. This included sending the Union Twelfth Corps to reoccupy

Harpers Ferry and the Sixth Corps to deploy along the Potomac on the Maryland shore opposite Boteler's Ford. The latter force, under General William Franklin, was ordered to open fire and inflict as much "damage as possible" on the Confederates. Perhaps sensing the possibility of a trap, McClellan further directed that they remain on the Maryland side of the Potomac until further ordered.[158]

Before the Sixth Corps could be deployed at the ford, it was diverted upstream to Williamsport. There, a Confederate force led by General J.E.B. Stuart drew Union attention to that sector. As a consequence, McClellan dispatched the Fifth Corps, under General Fitz John Porter, to Boteler's Ford. Porter sent Pleasonton's command back to the Sharpsburg area and then lined the C&O Canal and the river with sharpshooters and nineteen cannons under Colonel Henry Hunt of the Artillery Reserve.

Porter had the same discretionary orders as Franklin regarding crossing the river but sensed that the Confederates in his front were numerically weak. Indeed, only two small Confederate infantry brigades with some cavalry—fewer than six hundred men—guarded the ford, along with the forty-four cannons from Lee's Artillery Reserve placed there by chief of artillery General William Nelson Pendleton. Accordingly, Porter directed a task force of volunteers, about four hundred men from General George Morell's Division, to make a dash across the ford and "secure some of the enemy artillery." Around sundown, this force completely surprised the Confederates. The Rebels fled in panic, abandoning the forty-four cannons positioned there. In the darkness, the Union attackers did not realize the extent of their success and returned to the Maryland shore with only two captured guns, along with several caissons, forges and four hundred stand of arms.[159]

In the wake of this small disaster, a distraught General Pendleton mistakenly reported the loss of his entire artillery reserve to General Lee at about 1:00 a.m. on September 20 and sought reinforcements. Conversely, the Confederate retreat from the river convinced McClellan that an important opportunity loomed to further damage Lee's army. As a result, McClellan ordered Sykes's and Morell's Divisions, augmented by Pleasonton's cavalry and horse artillery, to cross the ford the next morning (September 20) and mount another attack.[160]

As word of Confederate concentrations at Williamsport reached McClellan, Pleasonton was ordered to send a large part of his force in response to the perceived threat. This left only half of his command and two batteries to support Porter. By 7:00 a.m. on the twentieth, Porter had

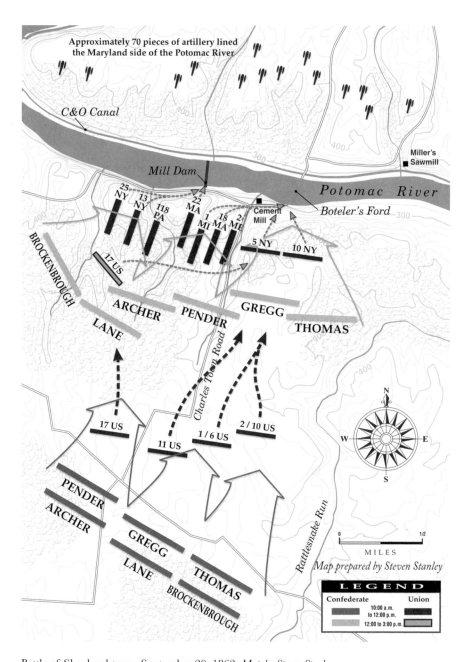

Approximately 70 pieces of artillery lined
the Maryland side of the Potomac River

C&O Canal

Mill Dam

Potomac River

Boteler's Ford

Miller's
Sawmill

Battle of Shepherdstown, September 20, 1862. *Map by Steven Stanley.*

directed his two divisions to begin crossing. Elements of Pleasonton's cavalry eventually joined this movement. About 9:00 a.m., three brigades from the division of General George Sykes reached the opposite shore and moved up Charlestown Road. Supporting Sykes was Colonel James Barnes's brigade from Morell's Division. Barnes deployed his command north of the ford on high bluffs overlooking the river. By 9:15 a.m., the head of Sykes's column had encountered Confederate infantry about three-quarters of a mile in from the river. What followed was one of the worst small-scale tactical debacles of the war. The action only lasted about an hour, yet it was a particularly bloody sixty minutes.[161]

Sykes soon discovered that he was not up against a small, disorganized Confederate rearguard but rather the entire division of Confederate general A.P. Hill, some three thousand strong. The Union troops were outnumbered nearly two to one. The previous night, Confederate artillery chief General William N. Pendleton had reported to Lee the loss of the entire artillery reserve. In response, General Thomas "Stonewall" Jackson personally set out to scout the area around the ford. He determined that the situation was not as bad as Pendleton had reported. Indeed, an enterprising Confederate officer, Major William Nelson, rescued most of the guns and had them moved to a safer location.[162]

In response to the emergency, Lee sent orders for Jackson to move his command to the river and repulse the Federals. He also directed Longstreet to deploy his troops along the Charlestown Pike in a defensive line. Jackson, meanwhile, on his own initiative and without hearing from Lee, directed three divisions to the river. A.P. Hill's Division, the least bloodied of the Confederate command since they had been at Harpers Ferry and took part in the tail end of the Battle of Sharpsburg, was sent forward to meet the enemy.

Sykes prudently withdrew his command back across the river to the Maryland shore. This left Barnes's Brigade of Morell's Division to face the Confederate attack alone. There were a total of four thousand Confederates and three thousand Federals on the field, but the major part of the fighting took place between three thousand Confederates and seventeen hundred Federals. Hill deployed his division at the intersection of the Charlestown Pike and Trough Road, about a mile from Boteler's Ford, forming it into two lines. Sweeping the Federals before them, despite stiff artillery fire from Union guns on the Maryland side, Hill forced Barnes to order a retreat.

In the midst of the chaos, the 118th Pennsylvania (the "Corn Exchange Regiment") found itself isolated and outflanked. This unit had been in service only a few weeks; most of its men had never seen combat, and they were armed with faulty weapons that malfunctioned that day. The results were sadly predictable. The Pennsylvanians panicked and made a mad rush for the river. Some fell from the bluffs above. Others sought refuge in the nearby cement mill and kilns. Soon, the river was filled with blue-coated bodies as the men of the 118th were shot down attempting to get back across the river.

Total Union losses in the battle were 363 (71 killed, 161 wounded, 131 captured or missing). The 118th Pennsylvania suffered the worst. Out of 737 men, 63 were killed, 101 wounded and 105 listed as either captured or missing. This was a total of 269 casualties, or approximately 36 percent of those engaged. Confederate casualties were 261 (30 killed and 321 wounded). The total for both sides, 624, made the Battle of Shepherdstown the bloodiest combat in what became the state of West Virginia.[163]

Jackson's quick action in getting troops on the scene saved the day for Lee. In the words of esteemed Antietam scholar Joseph Harsh, "For Stonewall Jackson it was a small gem of tactical execution. He reacted quickly and intelligently…with a minimum of force, Jackson achieved a complete victory…and ended any thought the Federals had of exploiting a confused Confederate army in retreat."

Once across the river, Lee positioned his army in the lower Shenandoah Valley along Opequon (pronounced o-PECK-in) Creek, in a line running from Bunker Hill, Virginia (now West Virginia), eastward to Berryville to let his soldiers rest and get resupplied. Lee had lost a fourth of his army at

Shepherdstown Battlefield as viewed from the North Shore of the Potomac. *Stephen J. Recker Collection.*

Sharpsburg. Now at the camps along the Opequon, thousands of stragglers drifted back to the ranks of the Army of Northern Virginia. Within two weeks of the battle, Lee's strength was up to 62,713 men. By October 20, nearly 80,000 filled the ranks.[164]

Meanwhile, McClellan had reconfigured his army's position, with the Second and Twelfth Corps forming his left at Harpers Ferry; his center, the Ninth Corps, around Antietam Furnace; the Fifth Corps posted around the town of Sharpsburg; the First Corps north of the town, camped on the battlefield; and the Sixth Corps forming McClellan's right in the vicinity of Bakersville and Williamsport. An anxious Lincoln came to visit the Army of the Potomac on October 1 and stayed for three days. During this visit, he prodded McClellan to take action and follow up on his victory at Antietam. However, "Little Mac" remained for the most part unresponsive to Lincoln's pleas.[165]

McClellan and Lincoln. *Antietam National Battlefield.*

On October 10, another embarrassing incident occurred to further diminish McClellan's competency in Lincoln's and the nation's eyes. J.E.B. Stuart, with a task force of about eighteen hundred cavalry, rode around the Army of the Potomac, raiding Chambersburg, Pennsylvania. Along the way, he took civilian hostages and livestock and destroyed the Cumberland Valley Railroad yards.[166]

On October 16–17, 1862, McClellan ordered a major reconnaissance-in-force. During the move back into Virginia, the Confederates destroyed several miles of the Baltimore & Ohio Railroad between Martinsburg and Harpers Ferry, rendering useless one of McClellan's best transportation networks. As Lee refitted his army, his Union counterpart was also getting reinforced.

Thinking that Lee might be pulling his army out of the lower Shenandoah, McClellan directed two separate columns to mount a reconnaissance-in-force into Jefferson County, (West) Virginia, to find out what the Rebels were up to. On October 16, General Andrew A. Humphreys crossed the Potomac River below Shepherdstown, at Boteler's Ford, with a six-thousand-man infantry force from the Fifth Corps, five hundred cavalry and six pieces of artillery. His objective was Kearneysville, a village located along the B&O and at the crossroads of highways that led from Charles Town and Martinsburg.

The second Union reconnaissance column was to march out of Harpers Ferry and head for Charles Town. It was led by General Winfield Scott Hancock, commander of the 1st Division of the Second Corps. Hancock had replaced General Israel B. Richardson, who was wounded during the attack on the Sunken Road and would die of his wounds on November 3. Hancock's force consisted of his own division and fifteen hundred men from other commands, for a total of about six thousand infantry, along with several hundred cavalry and four pieces of artillery.

The putting into motion of more than twelve thousand men was no doubt in response to a long letter from President Lincoln dated October 13, in which he pointed out to Little Mac that his army was actually closer to Richmond than Lee's was and that a rapid movement might sever the Confederates' line of communication with their capital. Lincoln then taunted his general, stating that if the troops of the Army of the Potomac could march as well as those of the enemy, Lee could be whipped. Both columns stayed in the field about two days. During that period, they skirmished with Confederate cavalry and infantry. A handful of casualties were incurred on both sides, and then both Union columns fell back to their point of origin.[167]

McClellan apparently was satisfied with his generals' reports of the whereabouts of Lee's army. Except for actions at Shepherdstown on

September 19 and 20, during Lee's withdrawal from Sharpsburg, the Union reconnaissance-in-force of October 16–17 marked the first aggressive action taken by Little Mac in the weeks following Antietam.

By now, any movements by McClellan were too little, too late for President Lincoln. On Sunday, October 26, the Army of the Potomac began crossing the Potomac at Berlin, Maryland, into Virginia. On November 7, McClellan received word that he was relieved of command. On November 10, the entire army was called out for an important event: its farewell review for General McClellan.

First Lieutenant George W. Welsh, Company A, 126th Pennsylvania, wrote a vivid account of McClellan's farewell:

> *On Tuesday morning we were ordered to turn out for review and it was stated that Gen'l McClellan had been relieved of his command and would take leave of the army. It was a most splendid sight. Our whole division was drawn up near the road and facing it. Away off to the right the cannon commenced booming, and cheer after cheer, from thousands announced the Commander's coming. In a short time he made his appearance with his Staff and Corps Commanders. The music struck up, the men presented arms, and George B. McClellan took leave of an army which loved him and which sadly saw his departure.*[168]

The various Confederate military incursions of the fall of 1862 had all failed. On October 4, more than four thousand Confederate soldiers became casualties in General Earl Van Dorn's failed attempt to secure the important railroad junction of Corinth, Mississippi. On October 8, the major battle to be fought on Kentucky soil during the war took place at Perryville. There, General Braxton Bragg's invasion of the Bluegrass State came to a halt. The next day, he began a tortuous withdrawal back to his base in Tennessee. William Loring's attempt to retake western Virginia also met with failure.[169]

Never again would the Confederacy have the will or military might to mount so many offensives as it did in the fall of 1862. The bloodiest and most decisive of these incursion was Lee's invasion of Maryland. His repulse back across the Potomac gave Lincoln the impetus to issue the "preliminary" Emancipation Proclamation. The final version came out on January 1, 1863.

Cynics and critics are quick to point out that this only freed slaves in those territories in rebellion: "All persons held as slaves within any state…in rebellion against the United States shall be then, thenceforward, and forever free." But even with its limitations, the proclamation had a profound effect on the institution of slavery. Esteemed Civil War–era scholar Edna Greene Medford has pointed out that "despite Confederate efforts to conceal news of the document from those in bondage, the enslaved population of the South soon learned by grapevine and through fragments of overheard conversation that their 'day of jubilee' had come." Soon, thousands of enslaved African Americans were voting with their feet, fleeing plantations in order to reach the nearest Union army camps.

In his definitive work, *Lincoln's Emancipation Proclamation: The End of Slavery in America*, Allen Guelzo poses the question, "Was Emancipation really a military asset? The answer had to be yes." Indeed, it drained the Confederacy of valuable slave labor used to construct fortifications and other duties that left white men free to shoulder a musket.

James McPherson has aptly pointed out that "the battle of Antietam and the Emancipation Proclamation had a signal impact abroad." The Emancipation Proclamation influenced both the largely antislavery England and France from intervening on behalf of the Confederacy. Now, the war had two aims: preserve the Union and end slavery.[170]

11

Future Generations Will Swell with Pride

A Union soldier passing over the battlefield in the summer of 1864 wrote, "At every stop the eye rests upon something to remind the traveler of that awful day of carnage." For years after the battle, it was a common sight to see human bones lying loose in gutters and fence corners. Erosion and the rooting of hogs had exposed many of the shallow graves, particularly of the Confederates. It was not uncommon to see hogs with human limbs in their mouths.

Government efforts to record what happened at Antietam began as early as 1867, when the U.S. War Department directed army cartographer Captain Nathanial Michler to supervise a survey of the battlefield and create a map of the battle, showing key terrain feature and troop movements. Michler's map was a precursor of continued War Department interest in the country's Civil War battlefields.[171]

By 1867, Union remains had been removed from the field and interred in the new Antietam National Cemetery. The Antietam National Cemetery was established by acts of the Maryland state legislature in 1864 and 1865. The original plan was to have Union and Confederate dead buried together in the same cemetery. However, this did not sit well with many Northern states, which had been asked to contribute funds. After much debate, the cemetery board decided that only Union soldiers would be permitted in the cemetery. The reinterment of Confederate dead occurred in 1870, when they were buried in Hagerstown's Washington Confederate Cemetery. Union bodies were exhumed from the battlefield in late 1866 and into 1867 by laborers and farmers, contracted out for about one dollar per day.[172]

Antietam National Cemetery dedication, September 17, 1867. *Antietam National Battlefield.*

On September 17, 1867, on the fifth anniversary of the battle, the Antietam National Cemetery was officially dedicated. President Andrew Johnson and other dignitaries were in attendance. Johnson was an unpopular president who had inherited the mantle of chief executive upon the assassination of Lincoln. His reconstruction policies were considered by many in the North to be too favorable toward the South. Accordingly, he was not received well by the audience at Antietam. Instead, he was subjected to some catcalls and boos. The *Hagerstown Torchlight and Herald* remarked, "Such was Mr. Johnson's reception by the fathers, mothers, brothers, sister, widows, orphans and surviving comrades of the sleeping heroes of Antietam, that it would have been better if he had stayed away." After some brief remarks, Johnson and his entourage hastily departed the ceremonies, leaving more popular "loyal" dignitaries to complete the program. In July 1879, the cemetery was transferred over to the jurisdiction of the U.S. War Department.[173]

Even before the U.S. government took an active role in developing the battlefield, local citizens and veterans were commemorating what had happened there on that bloody day in 1862. On the twenty-fifth anniversary of the battle in 1887, the veterans of the 20th New York Regiment dedicated a monument "in honor of their fallen comrades" at the Antietam National Cemetery. Other small monuments followed. In 1889, the survivors of Company A, 5th Maryland Regiment, purchased a plot of ground near Bloody Lane. There they would erect a modest monument in memory of their color-bearer and other fallen comrades. As monuments were erected,

Right: Dedication of the monument to the Private Soldier, September 17, 1880. *Stephen J. Recker Collection.*

Below: Veterans of the 20th New York Infantry at their monument. *Antietam National Battlefield.*

visitation to the site increased. The editor of the *Antietam Valley Review* noted in the September 30, 1892 issue, "Antietam battlefield has been visited within the past two weeks by thousands of veterans and their friends."[174]

The movement to preserve the major battlefields of the Civil War had as its genesis in the desire of aging veterans to remember the sacrifices that were made on these fields. Coupled with this was a desire for reconciliation. By this time, a large proportion of the members of Congress were Civil War veterans. Therefore, it was not hard to get them to appropriate funds to establish a number of major battlefields as National Battlefields. Antietam became the third of three such sites established in 1890 under the supervision of the U.S. War Department. Gettysburg and Chickamauga–Chattanooga were the others. Unfortunately, Antietam did not get the attention that these and subsequent battlefields would attract.[175]

While significant parcels of land were acquired at both Gettysburg and Chickamauga–Chattanooga, Davis's recommendation to the secretary of war was a minimalist approach to land acquisition at Antietam. This had far-reaching ramifications for the preservation of the battlefield, leaving most of it in private hands. Under this policy, which became known as the "Antietam Plan," strips of land conforming to battle lines and major battle features were acquired. Ironically, because of the rural nature of the surrounding landscape and Sharpsburg's isolated location—one that had been dictated more than a century before when it lost out to Hagerstown as the county seat—by the late twentieth century, Antietam remained the best-preserved battlefield in the East.[176]

One of the most important individuals connected with the creation of the Antietam National Battlefield Site (the word "Site" would be dropped in the latter part of the twentieth century) was Ezra Carman. After some political wrangling, Carman was appointed as the "historical expert" for the battlefield board. Carman was a veteran of Antietam, where he led the 13th New Jersey Regiment. He began his research just days after the battle. Over the years, Carman corresponded with scores of Antietam veterans, both blue and gray. As the historian for the battlefield board, he continued this process. Letters and maps were sent out to participants for them to mark where their particular units had fought. From this research, Carman developed troop movement maps and wrote the text for the iron tablets that were placed around the field. He also developed the tour road plan.[177]

Individual states and regimental associations continued to erect monuments on the field. In 1898, the Maryland General Assembly appropriated $12,500 to the soldiers of both armies that fought at

Antietam. The initial plan was to commemorate only Union participation, but Senator Norman C. Scott was influential in having the Confederates included. It is estimated that upwards of twenty-five thousand people attended the dedication on May 30, 1900. Attendees included President William McKinley, Secretary of War Elihu Root and former Confederate generals James Longstreet and Joseph Wheeler. It is the only monument on the battlefield that is dedicated to both sides.[178]

Ezra Carman, "Historical Expert" of the Antietam National Battlefield Board. *New York Public Library.*

The news that the government was helping to preserve the battlefield was greeted with enthusiasm by the people of Sharpsburg. In October 1894, the citizens of Sharpsburg organized the Antietam Battlefield Memorial Association. The local newspaper reported:

> *Our citizens are beginning to take a deep interest in the work of laying out this battlefield, and have it eventually pass into the hands of the government. Our town has always manifested a loyalty to the Union, and now we have an opportunity—a grand opportunity to demonstrate our patriotism and to show our deepest regard for the faith and work of the heroes now sleeping in Antietam National Cemetery.*

This show of support would be tried over the decades. Conflict erupted in the early part of the twentieth century over use of the park roads. Farmers, with their tractors and free-roaming cattle, wreaked havoc on the battlefield avenues. Superintendent Charles Adams received permission in May 1912 to forbid such traffic and livestock on the government thoroughfares. The

Superintendent Charles Adams, mudered on June 6, 1912, by a disgruntled local citizen. *Antietam National Battlefield.*

road controversy became a factor in a grudge against Adams, held by Sharpsburg resident Charles Benner. On the morning of June 6, 1912, Benner shot and killed Adams, leaving his body on a park roadway. The assassin then went home and turned the gun on himself.[179]

By the early part of the twentieth century, much had remained the same in the area, while much had changed. In July 1906, Fred Wilder Cross, the historical archivist for the Massachusetts State Military Archives, made the first of many trips to Antietam and other Civil War battlefields of the Eastern Theater. Cross made these working vacations, staying with local people and walking much of the field. He continued his travels for more than forty years. On July 6, 1903, he wrote, "The village of Sharpsburg…is little changed after the lapse of forty years. Its cobble streets and stout flagged sidewalks are the same which once resounded with the tramp of hostile armies…The East Wood like the West has disappeared. The Sunken Road looks like a grass grown ditch." Cross was seduced by the pristine state of the battlefield and wrote, "Antietam was one of the most interesting battlefields which I ever visited."[180]

Local guide O.T. Reilly, in his pictorial booklet published the same year as Cross's visit, provided a vivid picture of the Dunker Church:

> *Many bullet and shell marks show in the few remaining trees that stand near the church, one of the number has the entire top cut off by a shell. The few remaining trees that stand on the Antietam Battlefield can easily be pointed out, the limbs being very short and stubby caused by the ends being cut off by the shells and missiles of various kinds during the battle.*[181]

President Theodore Roosevelt at the dedication of the New Jersey State Monument, September 17, 1903. *Antietam National Battlefield.*

September 17, 1912, was the fiftieth anniversary of the battle. Although a commemorative event was held, it was very low key. Individual regimental associations held their reunions at different spots on the field. For example, forty-eight survivors of the 20th New York returned to the fields of the Mumma Farm, gathering by the small obelisk monument that marked the farthest advance of the regiment in the battle. That afternoon, three thousand people gathered in the National Cemetery for a ceremony.[182]

On September 17, 1920, the imposing New York State Monument was dedicated in the Mumma fields just east of Hagerstown Road. Approximately 250 veterans, a large proportion of whom fought at Antietam, attended.

Many of these old soldiers were in their eighties and nineties. Notable personalities in attendance included General Nelson Miles, a veteran of the Battle of Antietam and a famed Indian fighter in the post–Civil War West; and General John F. O'Ryan, commander of the 27th Division in France during World War I. Major Jacob Monath, superintendent of the Antietam National Battlefield, gave brief remarks accepting the monument on behalf of the United States government. Battlefield tramper Fred Cross termed it "the last great gathering of Civil War soldiers on this field."[183]

One of the most violent storms of the century hit southern Washington County on May 23, 1921. The major storm casualty on the Antietam Battlefield was the Dunker Church, which was leveled. The War Department attempted to purchase the site with plans to rebuild the battlefield shrine. However, the requested appropriation of $6,200 was turned down by the department's budget office. The great landmark would not be rebuilt for another thirty-nine years. For years, the site remained just a pile of rubble. The heirs of the Mumma family regained control of the church site. The property and the wreckage were sold at public auction in the summer of 1924. Elmer Boyer, a Sharpsburg grocer, purchased the ruins for $805 and placed all of it in storage.[184]

During the first three decades of the twentieth century, there was much disagreement in Congress as to what agency should manage the country's National Battlefields. Many felt that the War Department had fallen down in its stewardship role as caretaker of these sites. Conversely, many in Congress and government were dubious when the idea of the placing the National Park Service (NPS) in charge of the battlefields was raised.

As early as 1917, Horace Albright, assistant director of the fledging new agency, had attempted to secure passage of an act that would transfer the national battlefield to the NPS. When Albright became director in 1929, he continued his campaign and gained supporters in both the War and Interior Departments. His lobbying efforts were finally rewarded, and the issue was settled in 1933 with the election of President Franklin D. Roosevelt. One of the first steps taken by FDR was to reorganize the executive branch of government. One of the many changes that took place was the placing of the military parks under the National Park Service.[185]

Antietam National Battlefield Site came originally under the jurisdiction of Gettysburg National Military Park, which was to provide oversight and administrative staff support. On October 10, 1933, John Kyd Beckenbaugh, a native of Washington County and nephew of Confederate staff officer Henry Kyd Douglas, was appointed superintendent of Antietam National

Battlefield Site. Beckenbaugh ran the daily operations of the park. He was not able to report for duty until January 10, 1934, and in the interim operations were run by National Cemetery superintendent Clarence Nett. (The cemetery was still managed separately.).[186]

However, funds were provided through emergency allotments and Civil Works Administration Projects for a "Historical Survey Project" and a "Labor Project" to clean up neglected parts of the site. The Historical Survey team, composed of young college students, represented the first extensive research and collection of data since the Carman period of the 1890s. Indeed, most of the interpretive improvements and land development and acquisition plans that came about in the 1940s were based on this research.

Superintendent John Kyd Beckenbaugh (1933–1940). *Antietam National Battlefield.*

Beckenbaugh saw the need for an improvement program at Antietam National Battlefield and used the findings of the CWA Historical Survey Team to justify it at an estimated cost of $90,000. This included purchase of sections of Bloody Lane, the Smoketown Road and the Dunker Church site. The report also recommend replacing the approximately thirteen miles of modern park fencing with the types that existed at the time of the battle. While the park service made plans to upgrade and restore the site, a major event was to occur that would have the greatest impact on the area since the battle. This was the seventy-fifth anniversary of the Battle of Antietam.[187]

On September 17, 1937, the seventy-fifth anniversary of the Battle of Antietam was commemorated with patriotic speeches by notables, including President Franklin D. Roosevelt, and a battle reenactment at Bloody Lane featuring about two thousand men from the District of Columbia, Maryland, Pennsylvania and Virginia National Guards. President Roosevelt

Superintendent Beckenbaugh with members of the United Daughters of the Confederacy at the dedication of the Lee's Headquarters Monument. *Antietam National Battlefield.*

arrived at 12:00 p.m., his motorcade riding down the tour road paralleling Bloody Lane. Bleachers, with a five-thousand-seat capacity, were erected on a nearby hill overlooking Bloody Lane. An estimated fifty thousand people attended, and Superintendent Beckenbaugh termed it "the largest peace-time crowd ever gathered in this section." The seventy-fifth anniversary generated public interest in the battlefield and its preservation.[188]

The seventy-fifth anniversary was a boon to visitation. More than seventy-seven thousand people came to Antietam in 1937, in large part due to the anniversary festivities. By and large, during the 1930s and into the '40s, visitation averaged around twenty thousand per year.[189]

Upon the death of Superintendent Beckenbaugh in 1940, the park came once again under the supervision of Gettysburg. Beckenbaugh had accomplished much in park improvements during his tenure. Planning for the park continued unabated after Beckenbaugh's passing. In August 1941, just four months before Pearl Harbor, a "Master Plan" was approved for Antietam. It called for much of what had been suggested in the earlier survey. World War II and the decline in visitation because of gas rationing (7,687 visitors in 1943), along with a federal government now on a war path, brought much park development at Antietam to a halt. At the end of the war, it looked like improvements could continue at the battlefield, but the Korean War put another crimp in the park budget. However, the park's slow fiscal climb out of the cutbacks of two wars were about to come to an end.

Future Generations Will Swell with Pride

Above: President Franklin D. Roosevelt at the podium set up at Bloody Lane during the seventy-fifth anniversary of the battle. *Antietam National Battlefield.*

Right: An elderly yet spry Confederate veteran at the seventy-fifth anniversary. *Antietam National Battlefield.*

Union veterans at the National Cemetery Lodge during the seventy-fifth anniversary. *Antietam National Battlefield.*

A new federal initiative was about to give Antietam National Battlefield and other park services a shot in the arm.[190]

Two events put Antietam National Battlefield on the map in the 1960s: an NPS initiative dubbed "Mission 66" and the Civil War Centennial. The challenge of instituting an NPS version of the Marshall Plan was taken up in the early 1950s with ardor by new NPS director Conrad Wirth. His plan to restore the parks was modeled after strategies used by agencies involved in major development projects such as the Army Corps of Engineers and Bureau of Public Roads. Because of the immensity of dam and highway projects, such agencies were able to get funding packages spanning several years. Conversely, small projects proposed by the NPS on an annual basis tended to be easily cut when Congress needed to wield its budget-cutting axe. Accordingly, Wirth proposed an "all-inclusive, long-term program" for the NPS. Thus was born Mission 66.[191]

The plan caught the ear of President Dwight D. Eisenhower. Soon, "Ike" contacted the secretary of the interior for a briefing on the status of the parks. Wirth formed committees in the Washington office to plan Mission 66 and lobbied individual members of Congress. Finally, at a cabinet meeting in January 1956, he was able to present Mission 66 to President Eisenhower, gaining firm support for the ten-year project. Mission 66 included extensive construction and development, as well as major staff increases, particularly for interpretation, maintenance and law enforcement. Hundreds of projects were implemented under Mission 66, including rehabilitation and construction of roads, construction of parking areas and restoration of historic buildings, to name a few. Approximately 114 new visitors' centers were also constructed, among them the Antietam National Battlefield's.[192]

In the late fall of 1962, the building was completed. It was opened to the public in January 1963. Meanwhile, the National Park Service, in cooperation with other organizations, planned a more than two-week commemoration of the battle. This event would bring more people to Antietam than any other event since the seventy-fifth anniversary of 1937. As early as December 1956, park officials took part in a meeting with about twenty other organizations, spearheaded by the Washington County Historical Society, to form the Antietam Centennial Committee. The "Grand Re-Enactment of the Battle of Antietam," as it was called,

A reeanctor, 9th New York, Hawkin's Zouaves, at the 100th anniversary of the battle reenactment. *Ted Alexander Collection.*

was held at 2:00 p.m., on September 15 and 16, 1962. The event focused on the Bloody Lane phase of the battle and was held primarily in the lane and the adjacent fields of the Roulette and Mumma Farms. Around two thousand reenactors from twenty-one states and the District of Columbia took part in the two-day affair.

Fifty thousand visitors were projected to descend on the battlefield for the reenactment. Only about eighteen thousand actually attended, ten thousand on Saturday and eight thousand on Sunday. The other great disappointment was the absence of any former or sitting U.S. president. Former President Eisenhower had said he might attend but then decided not to make the drive down from his Gettysburg farm. President John F. Kennedy also declined an invitation to attend. The Antietam reenactment was the last such event held at

Confederate reenactors, 100th anniversary reenactment. *Ted Alexander Collection.*

100th anniversary reenactment held on Mumma Farm, September 1962. *Ted Alexander Collection.*

a National Battlefield. Safety and preservation issues, along with the question of whether it was appropriate to have reenactments on hallowed ground, caused the National Park Service to prohibit further reenactments on NPS property.[193]

Three major Mission 66 projects were completed for the 100th anniversary of the battle. Two of them—the Burnside Bridge overlook and the visitors' center—received mixed reactions from the public. By far, the least controversial and obtrusive project was the reconstruction of the Dunker Church. The long years of planning to reconstruct the church came to an end with the advent of the Civil War Centennial. The Washington County Committee for the Commemoration of the Centennial of the Battle of Antietam made the reconstruction a high priority. Maryland governor Millard Tawes, honorary chairman of the Maryland Civil War Centennial Commission, was a big supporter of the effort and arranged for $35,000 of state funding for the project. The park service would supervise the reconstruction and maintenance of the church.

By the Fourth of July, the church was officially opened to the public. The first public visitor to enter the reconstructed Dunker Church was Miss Ruth

Otto, who had attended services there as a child. Her father, John, had been the last full-time pastor, and her great uncle was Samuel Mumma, the man who donated the land for the church.[194]

In April, President John F. Kennedy visited the Antietam National Battlefield. The president and his entourage, including his brother, Senator Edward Kennedy, and his wife, Joan, rode via helicopter in nine minutes from nearby Camp David, landing at 11:45 a.m. near Burnside Bridge. An avid Civil War buff, Kennedy toured the park in a white convertible with park historian Robert Lagaman. The group stayed outdoors for the entire tour and did not enter the visitor center.[195]

In 1979, the park purchased and restored four battle panoramas of Antietam by James Hope. Hope had been at the battle as a captain in the 2nd Vermont Infantry and was a landscape artist. He made sketches of the battle at the time and later used these as the basis for large panoramas, which he displayed in his gallery in Watkins Glen, New York, after the war. These panoramas are now on display in the museum of the Antietam Visitor Center. They offer graphic and realistic images of the battle.[196]

In September 1987, the park commemorated the 125th anniversary of the Battle of Antietam. Thousands of visitors attended lectures, Civil War music concerts, ranger- led walking tours and costumed interpretive programs such as cannon firing and infantry tactical demonstrations.

During this period, two major events were introduced. The Maryland Symphony Salute to Independence is held on the Saturday closest to the Fourth of July. Crowds in excess of forty thousand attend this event, featuring a concert of patriotic airs that concludes with the "1812 Overture" and a spectacular fireworks display. The Annual Memorial Illumination is held the first Saturday in December. More than one thousand volunteers place twenty-three thousand luminaries (candles in bags of sand) over the center of the battlefield to represent the casualties of America's bloodiest day. More than ten thousand visitors are drawn to this, one of the most moving events in the United States.[197]

In October 2000, I had the sad task of receiving a call from the Veterans Administration concerning a fallen American hero. The caller was asking how to facilitate the burial of a recent military casualty in the Antietam National Cemetery. That casualty was nineteen-year-old Fireman Apprentice Patrick Roy, who was killed in the terrorist attack on the USS *Cole*. Roy was a native of nearby Keedysville and as a youth had helped place flowers on the graves at Antietam National Cemetery with his classmates on Memorial Day.

Officially, the cemetery had been closed to any further burial following the Korean War. I contacted the acting superintendent on this matter, and he

Bloody Lane at sunset. *Courtesy of Scott Anderson.*

immediately got hold of Superintendent John Howard, who was on vacation at the time. Howard wasted no time in cutting through all the bureaucratic red tape to facilitate having Fireman Roy, one of the first casualties of the War on Terror, laid to rest in Antietam National Cemetery.[198]

Fast-forward a little less than a year to September 11, 2001. The terror attacks that day racked up a body count that rivaled Antietam. The park was deluged with calls from the media asking which event was the bloodiest day in American history. For the next few weeks, thousands of people descended on the battlefield to reflect, contemplate and mourn what had just befallen the nation, using Antietam as their emotional vessel.

Antietam National Battlefield continues to be a site for education, reflection and commemoration. It remains one of the great yet terrible battles of the Civil War. In 1897, General Ezra Carman, the historian for the Antietam Battlefield Board, received a letter from James Dinkins, a Confederate veteran of the battle. The letter concerned troop movements and locations. Carman was preparing the text for the cast-iron tablets that are so familiar to visitors. In the letter's conclusion, Dinkins inadvertently penned a fitting tribute to the men of both armies that fought at Antietam: "Future generations looking at the markers will swell with pride as they read of the heroic character of their ancestors, and they will also have more appreciation of peace."

Appendix

Forlorn Hopes

C ritics of George B. McClellan's generalship at Antietam usually cite his failure to commit more than twenty-five thousand reserves to the battle. These troops, they say, were never used and could have been sent in to strike the final blow against Lee's weak line on Sharpsburg Ridge. Who exactly were these reserves? A major reserve component for McClellan was the Fifth Corps under Major General Fitz John Porter. By September 18, this corps numbered more than ten thousand men with three divisions. It had suffered stiff casualties at Second Manassas. Fewer than four thousand troops were committed on September 17, mostly Sykes's small regular division, which probed the Confederate center on Cemetery Hill. Porter's 1st Division, under Major General George W. Morell, was composed of three brigades of regiments with a mixed record of combat experience, including new units such as the totally green 118th Pennsylvania (Corn Exchange) Regiment and the 20th Maine, which had left its home state for service just two weeks before. Humphrey's Division was organized on September 12 and then forced to march to the field, arriving there on September 18. This third division had two brigades of Pennsylvanians, mostly nine-month units that had been in service for a few weeks.

Porter suffered 130 casualties at Antietam. This low body count no doubt influenced McClellan's critics in their assessment that he had thousands of fresh troops in reserve.

The other so-called reserve of the Army of the Potomac was the Sixth Corps under Major General William B. Franklin. They arrived near McClellan's headquarters about 10:00 a.m., having marched from Pleasant

Valley, and were across the Antietam Creek on the Union right before noon. The major component of this corps to see action was Colonel William H. Irwin's Brigade. About 1:00 p.m., following the collapse of the Rebel line in Bloody Lane, this command, forming the left flank of the corps, attacked the Confederate line around the Dunker Church.

Heavy Confederate musketry and canister stopped Irwin's advance and left 342 men of the Sixth Corps killed, wounded or missing. No further attacks were made by the Sixth Corps. That afternoon, both Sumner and McClellan had been convinced by the aggressiveness of the Confederates around the Dunker Church that more attacks against that sector would be foolish. General Franklin complied. The right flank of the Sixth Corps, Slocum's Division, in the vicinity of the Cornfield and East Woods, would suffer 68 men killed and wounded that afternoon, mostly from Confederate cannon fire. One of the dead was a thirteen-year-old drummer boy in the 49th Pennsylvania, Charlie King. He was the youngest soldier killed in action during the war.

Could the Fifth Corps, with its many green nine-month soldiers, and the Sixth Corps, which had lost fewer than five hundred men, have made a difference? This is a question that will continue to intrigue students of the Battle of Antietam and be the source of endless debate for years to come.

That afternoon, Robert E. Lee was thinking both defensively and offensively. While he worried about the collapse of his weakened right flank, he proposed that a task force, led by Jeb Stuart, explore the feasibility of turning the Union right flank. Accordingly, Stuart gathered twenty-six hundred cavalry, two regiments of infantry and eight rifled cannons from four separate Confederate batteries and marched on a circuitous route behind Nicodemus Heights to the northwest and then to the east opposite the Hagerstown Pike. The strength of the Union right soon became evident as the massed guns of the First Corps blasted the advance of Stuart's recon force, causing him to call off any further movement in that direction.

The last Union attempt to strike the Confederate center took place about 5:30 p.m., when Irwin, who was possibly drunk, ordered the 7th Maine to attack the reformed Confederate line at the Piper Farm. The results were sadly predictable. Around 180 men went into the attack, and only 90 returned.

Organization of the Army of the Potomac at Antietam

Major General George Brinton McClellan, Commanding

Escort
Captain James B. McIntyre
Independent Company, Oneida Cavalry (New York)
Company A, 4th U.S. Cavalry
Company E, 4th U.S. Cavalry

Volunteer Engineer Brigade[199]
Brigadier General Daniel P. Woodbury
15th New York Engineers
50th New York Engineers

Regular Engineer Battalion
Captain James C. Duane

Provost Guard
Major William H. Wood
Companies E, F, H and K, 2nd U.S. Cavalry
Companies A, D, F and G, 8th U.S. Infantry
Company G, 19th U.S. Infantry
Company H, 19th U.S. Infantry

Headquarters Guard
Major Granville O. Haller
Sturges's Rifles (Illinois)[200]
93rd New York Infantry

Quartermaster's Guard
Companies B, C, H and I, 1st U.S. Cavalry

First Corps
Major General Joseph Hooker (w)
Brigadier General George Gordon Meade

Escort
Companies A, B, I and K, 2nd New York Cavalry

1ST DIVISION
Brigadier General Abner Doubleday

1st Brigade
Colonel Walter Phelps Jr.
22nd New York
24th New York
30th New York
84th New York
2nd United States Sharpshooters

2nd Brigade
Lieutenant Colonel J. William Hofmann
7th Indiana
76th New York
95th New York
56th Pennsylvania

3rd Brigade
Brigadier General Marsena R. Patrick
21st New York
23rd New York
35th New York
80th New York

4th Brigade
Brigadier General John Gibbon
19th Indiana
2nd Wisconsin
6th Wisconsin
7th Wisconsin

1st Division/First Corps Artillery
Captain J. Albert Monroe
1st Battery, New Hampshire Light Artillery
Battery D, 1st Rhode Island Light Artillery
Battery L, 1st New York Light Artillery
Battery B, 4th United States Artillery

2ND DIVISION
Brigadier General James Brewerton Ricketts

1st Brigade
Brigadier General Abram Duryea
Colonel Peter Lyle
97th New York
104th New York
105th New York
107th Pennsylvania

2nd Brigade
Colonel William A. Christian

26th New York
94th New York
88th Pennsylvania
90th Pennsylvania

3rd Brigade

Brigadier General George Lucas Hartsuff (w)
Colonel Richard Coulter
16th Maine[201]
12th Massachusetts
13th Massachusetts
83rd New York
11th Pennsylvania

2nd Division/First Corps Artillery

Battery F, 1st Pennsylvania Light Artillery
Battery C, Pennsylvania Light Artillery

3RD DIVISION

Brigadier General George Gordon Meade
Brigadier General Truman Seymour

1st Brigade

Brigadier General Truman Seymour
Colonel R. Biddle Roberts
1st Pennsylvania Reserves
2nd Pennsylvania Reserves
5th Pennsylvania Reserves
6th Pennsylvania Reserves
13th Pennsylvania Reserves

2nd Brigade

Colonel Albert L. Magilton

3rd Pennsylvania Reserves
4th Pennsylvania Reserves
7th Pennsylvania Reserves
8th Pennsylvania Reserves

3rd Brigade

Lieutenant Colonel Robert Anderson
9th Pennsylvania Reserves
10th Pennsylvania Reserves
11th Pennsylvania Reserves
12th Pennsylvania Reserves

3rd Division/First Corps Artillery

Battery A, 1st Pennsylvania Light Artillery
Battery B, 1st Pennsylvania Light Artillery
Battery G, 1st Pennsylvania Light Artillery[202]
Battery C, 5th United States Artillery

SECOND CORPS
Major General Edwin Vose Sumner

ESCORT
Company D, 6th New York Cavalry
Company K 6th New York Cavalry

1ST DIVISION
Major General Israel B. Richardson (mw)
Brigadier General Winfield Scott Hancock

1st Brigade
Brigadier General John C. Caldwell
5th New Hampshire
7th New York
61st New York
64th New York
81st Pennsylvania

2nd Brigade
Brigadier General Thomas Meagher
29th Massachusetts
63rd New York
69th New York
88th New York

3rd Brigade
Colonel John Rutter Brooke
2nd Delaware
52nd New York
57th New York
66th New York
53rd Pennsylvania

1st Division/Second Corps Artillery
Battery B, 1st New York Light Artillery
Batteries A & C, 4th United States Artillery

2ND DIVISION
Major General John Sedgwick (w)
Brigadier General Oliver Otis Howard

1st Brigade
Brigadier General Willis Gorman
Colonel Joshua T. Owen
Colonel DeWitt C. Baxter

2nd Brigade
Brigadier General Oliver Otis Howard

15th Massachusetts	69th Pennsylvania
1st Minnesota	71st Pennsylvania
34th New York	72nd Pennsylvania
82nd New York	106th Pennsylvania

1st Company, Massachusetts Sharpshooters
2nd Company, Minnesota Sharpshooter

3rd Brigade
Brigadier General Napoleon J. T. Dana (w)
Colonel Norman Hall
19th Massachusetts
20th Massachusetts
7th Michigan
42nd New York
59th New York

2nd Division/Second Corps Artillery
Battery A, 1st Rhode Island Light Artillery
Battery I, 1st United States Artillery

3RD DIVISION
Brigadier General William Henry French

1st Brigade
Brigadier General Nathan Kimball
14th Indiana
8th Ohio
132nd Pennsylvania
7th West Virginia

2nd Brigade
Colonel Dwight Morris
14th Connecticut
108th New York
130th Pennsylvania

3rd Brigade
Brigadier General Max Weber (w)
Colonel John W. Andrews
1st Delaware
5th Maryland
4th New York

Unattached Second Corps Artillery
Battery G, 1st New York Light Artillery

Battery B, 1st Rhode Island Light Artillery
Battery G, 1st Rhode Island Light Artillery

FIFTH CORPS
Major General Fitz-John Porter

ESCORT
1st Maine Cavalry (detachment)

1ST DIVISION
Major General George Webb Morell

1st Brigade
Colonel James Barnes
2nd Maine
18th Massachusetts
22nd Massachusetts
1st Michigan
13th New York
25th New York
118th Pennsylvania
2nd Company, Massachusetts Sharpshooters

2nd Brigade
Brigadier General Charles Griffin
2nd District of Columbia
9th Massachusetts
32nd Massachusetts
4th Michigan
14th New York
62nd Pennsylvania

3rd Brigade
Colonel T.B.W. Stockton
20th Maine
16th Michigan
12th New York
17th New York
44th New York
83rd Pennsylvania
Brady's Company, Michigan Sharpshooters

Sharpshooters
1st United States Sharpshooters

1st Division/Fifth Corps Artillery
Battery C, Massachusetts Light Artillery
Battery C, 1st Rhode Island Light Artillery
Battery D, 5th United States Artillery

2ND DIVISION
Brigadier General George Sykes

1st Brigade
Lieutenant Colonel Robert C. Buchanan
3rd United States Infantry
4th United States Infantry
12th United States Infantry, 1st Battalion
12th United States Infantry, 2nd Battalion
14th United States Infantry, 1st Battalion
14th United States Infantry, 2nd Battalion

2nd Brigade
Major Charles S. Lovell
1st & 6th United States Infantry
2nd & 10th United States Infantry
11th United States Infantry
17th United States Infantry

3rd Brigade
Colonel Gouverneur K. Warren
5th New York
10th New York

2nd Division/Fifth Corps Artillery
Batteries E & G, 1st United States Artillery
Battery I, 5th United States Artillery
Battery K, 5th United States Artillery

3RD DIVISION
Brigadier General Andrew Atkinson Humphreys

1st Brigade
Brigadier General Erastus B. Tyler
91st Pennsylvania
126th Pennsylvania
129th Pennsylvania
134th Pennsylvania

2nd Brigade
Colonel Peter H. Allabach
123rd Pennsylvania
131st Pennsylvania
133rd Pennsylvania
155th Pennsylvania

3rd Division/Fifth Corps Artillery
Captain Lucius N. Robinson
Battery C, 1st New York Light Artillery
Battery L, 1st Ohio Light Artillery

Fifth Corps Reserve Artillery
Lieutenant Colonel William Hays
Battery A, 1st Battalion New York Light Artillery
Battery B, 1st Battalion New York Light Artillery
Battery C, 1st Battalion New York Light Artillery
Battery D, 1st Battalion New York Light Artillery
5th Battery, New York Light Artillery
Battery K, 1st United States Artillery
Battery G, 4th United States Artillery

SIXTH CORPS
Major General William B. Franklin

ESCORT
Companies B & G, 6th Pennsylvania Cavalry

1ST DIVISION
Major General Henry Warner Slocum

1st Brigade
Colonel Alfred T.A. Torbert
1st New Jersey
2nd New Jersey
3rd New Jersey
4th New Jersey

2nd Brigade
Colonel Joseph J. Bartlett
5th Maine
16th New York
27th New York
96th Pennsylvania

3rd Brigade
Brigadier General John Newton
18th New York
31st New York
32nd New York
95th Pennsylvania

1st Division/Sixth Corps Artillery
Captain Emory Upton
Battery A, Maryland Light Artillery
Battery A, Massachusetts Light Artillery
Battery A, New Jersey Light Artillery
Battery D, 2nd United States Artillery

2ND DIVISION
Major General William Farrar Smith

1st Brigade
Brigadier General Winfield Scott Hancock
Colonel Amasa Cobb
6th Maine
43rd New York
49th Pennsylvania
137th Pennsylvania
5th Wisconsin

2nd Brigade
Brigadier General William T.H. Brooks

2nd Vermont
3rd Vermont
4th Vermont
5th Vermont
6th Vermont

3rd Brigade
Colonel William H. Irwin
7th Maine
20th New York
33rd New York
49th New York
77th New York

2nd Division/Sixth Corps Artillery
Captain Romeyn Beck Ayres
Battery B, Maryland Light Artillery
1st Battery, New York Light Artillery
Battery F, 5th United States Artillery

FOURTH CORPS

1ST DIVISION[203]
Major General Darius Nash Couch

1st Brigade
Brigadier General Charles Devens Jr.
7th Massachusetts
10th Massachusetts
36th New York
2nd Rhode Island

2nd Division
Brigadier General Albion P. Howe
62nd New York
93rd Pennsylvania
98th Pennsylvania
102nd Pennsylvania
139th Pennsylvania

3rd Brigade
Brigadier General John Cochrane
65th New York
67th New York
122nd New York
23rd Pennsylvania
61st Pennsylvania
82nd Pennsylvania

1st Division/Fourth Corps Artillery
Third Battery, New York Light Artillery
Battery C, 1st Pennsylvania Light Artillery
Battery D, 1st Pennsylvania Light Artillery
Battery G, 2nd United States Artillery

NINTH CORPS
Major General Ambrose E. Burnside[204]
Brigadier General Jacob Dolson Cox

ESCORT
Company G, 1st Maine Cavalry

1ST DIVISION
Brigadier General Orlando Bolivar Willcox

1st Brigade
Colonel Benjamin C. Christ
28th Massachusetts
17th Michigan
79th New York
50th Pennsylvania

2nd Brigade
Colonel Thomas Welsh
8th Michigan
46th New York
45th Pennsylvania
100th Pennsylvania

1st Division/Ninth Corps Artillery
8th Battery, Massachusetts Light Artillery
Battery E, 2nd United States Artillery

2ND DIVISION
Brigadier General Samuel Davis Sturgis

1ˢᵗ Brigade
Brigadier General James Nagle
2ⁿᵈ Maryland
6ᵗʰ New Hampshire
9ᵗʰ New Hampshire
48ᵗʰ Pennsylvania

2ⁿᵈ Brigade
Colonel Edward Ferrero
21ˢᵗ Massachusetts
35ᵗʰ Massachusetts
51ˢᵗ New York
51ˢᵗ Pennsylvania

2ⁿᵈ Division/Ninth Corps Artillery
Battery D, Pennsylvania Light Artillery
Battery E, 4ᵗʰ United States Artillery

3ᴿᴰ DIVISION
Brigadier General Isaac Peace Rodman (mw)

1ˢᵗ Brigade
Colonel Harrison S. Fairchild
9ᵗʰ New York
89ᵗʰ New York
103ʳᵈ New York

2ⁿᵈ Brigade
Colonel Edward Harland
8ᵗʰ Connecticut
11ᵗʰ Connecticut
16ᵗʰ Connecticut
4ᵗʰ Rhode Island

3ʳᵈ Division/Ninth Corps Artillery
Battery A, 5ᵗʰ United States Artillery

4ᵀᴴ DIVISION
Colonel Eliakim P. Scammon

1ˢᵗ Brigade
Colonel Hugh Ewing
12ᵗʰ Ohio
23ʳᵈ Ohio
30ᵗʰ Ohio
1ˢᵗ Battery, Ohio Light Artillery
Gilmore's Company, West Virginia
  Cavalry
Harrison's Company, West Virginia
  Cavalry

2ⁿᵈ Brigade
Colonel George Crook
11ᵗʰ Ohio
28ᵗʰ Ohio
36ᵗʰ Ohio
Schambeck's Co., Chicago
  Dragoons
Simmond's Battery, Kentucky
  Light Artillery

Unattached Ninth Corps Units
6th New York Cavalry (8 Companies)
3rd Independent Company, Ohio Cavalry
Batteries L & M, 3rd United States Artillery

TWELFTH CORPS
Major General Joseph K.F. Mansfield (mw)
Brigadier General Alpheus Williams

ESCORT
Company L, 1st Michigan Cavalry

1ST DIVISION
Brigadier General Alpheus Williams
Brigadier General Samuel Wylie Crawford (w)
Brigadier General George Henry Gordon

1st Brigade
Brigadier General Samuel Wylie Crawford
Colonel Joseph F. Knipe
5th Connecticut[205]
10th Maine
28th New York
46th Pennsylvania
124th Pennsylvania
125th Pennsylvania
128th Pennsylvania

2nd Brigade
Brigadier General George H. Gordon
Colonel Thomas H. Ruger
27th Indiana
2nd Massachusetts
13th New Jersey
107th New York
Pennsylvania Zouaves D'Afrique
3rd Wisconsin

2ND DIVISION
Brigadier General George Sears Greene

1st Brigade
Lieutenant Colonel Hector Tyndale (w)
Major Orrin J. Crane
5th Ohio
7th Ohio
29th Ohio[206]
66th Ohio
28th Pennsylvania

2nd Brigade
Colonel Henry J. Stainrook

3rd Maryland
102nd New York
109th Pennsylvania[207]
111th Pennsylvania

3<u>rd</u> Brigade
Colonel William B. Goodrich (k)
Lieutenant Colonel Jonathan Austin
3rd Delaware
Purnell Legion (Maryland)
60th New York
78th New York

TWELFTH CORPS ARTILLERY
Captain Clermont L. Best
4th Battery, Maine Light Artillery
6th Battery, Maine Light Artillery
Battery M, 1st New York Light Artillery
10th Battery, New York Light Artillery
Battery E, Pennsylvania Light Artillery
Battery F, Pennsylvania Light Artillery
Battery F, 4th United States Artillery

CAVALRY DIVISION
Brigadier General Alfred Pleasonton

1<u>st</u> Brigade
Major Charles J. Whiting
5th United States Cavalry
6th United States Cavalry

2<u>nd</u> Brigade
Colonel John F. Farnsworth
8th Illinois Cavalry
3rd Indiana Cavalry
1st Massachusetts Cavalry

3<u>rd</u> Brigade
Colonel Richard H. Rush
4th Pennsylvania Cavalry
6th Pennsylvania Cavalry

4<u>th</u> Brigade
Colonel Andrew T. McReynolds
1st New York Cavalry
12th Pennsylvania Cavalry

5<u>th</u> Brigade
Colonel Benjamin F. Davis
8th New York Cavalry
3rd Pennsylvania Cavalry

Artillery/Cavalry Division
Battery A, 2ⁿᵈ United States Artillery
Batteries B & L, 2ⁿᵈ United States Artillery
Battery M, 2ⁿᵈ United States Artillery
Batteries C & G, 3ʳᵈ United States Artillery

Unattached Units/Cavalry
1ˢᵗ Maine Cavalry[208]
15ᵗʰ Pennsylvania Cavalry

ORGANIZATION OF THE ARMY OF NORTHERN VIRGINIA AT ANTIETAM

General Robert E. Lee, Commanding

LONGSTREET'S CORPS
Major General James Longstreet

MᶜLAWS'S DIVISION
Major General Lafayette McLaws

Kershaw's Brigade
Brigadier General Joseph Kershaw
2ⁿᵈ South Carolina
3ʳᵈ South Carolina
7ᵗʰ South Carolina
8ᵗʰ South Carolina

Cobb's Brigade
Brigadier General Howell Cobb
Lieutenant Colonel C.C. Sanders
Lieutenant Colonel William McRae
16ᵗʰ Georgia
24ᵗʰ Georgia
Cobb's (Georgia) Legion
15ᵗʰ North Carolina

Semmes's Brigade
Brigadier General Paul Semmes
10th Georgia
53rd Georgia
15th Virginia
32nd Virginia

Barksdale's Brigade
Brigadier General William Barksdale
13th Mississippi
17th Mississippi
18th Mississippi
21st Mississippi

Artillery
Major S.P. Hamilton
Colonel H.C. Cabell
Manly's (North Carolina) Battery
Pulaski (Georgia) Artillery
Richmond (Fayette) Artillery
Richmond Howitzers (1st Company)
Troup (Georgia) Artillery

ANDERSON'S DIVISION
Major General Richard H. Anderson

Wilcox's Brigade
Colonel Alfred Cumming
8th Alabama
9th Alabama
10th Alabama
11th Alabama

Mahone's Brigade
Colonel William A. Parham
6th Virginia
12th Virginia
16th Virginia
41st Virginia
61st Virginia

Featherston's Brigade
Colonel Carnot Posey
12th Mississippi
16th Mississippi
19th Mississippi
2nd Mississippi Battalion

Armistead's Brigade
Brigadier General Lewis Armistead
9th Virginia
14th Virginia
38th Virginia
53rd Virginia
57th Virginia

Pryor's Brigade
Brigadier General Roger A. Pryor
14th Alabama
2nd Florida
8th Florida
3rd Virginia

Wright's Brigade
Brigadier General Ambrose R. Wright
44th Alabama
3rd Georgia
22nd Georgia
48th Georgia

Artillery
Major John Saunders
Donaldsonville (Louisiana) Artillery (Maurin's Battery)
Huger's (Virginia) Battery
Moorman's (Virginia) Battery
Thompson's (Grimes's Virginia) Battery

JONES'S DIVISION
Brigadier General David R. Jones

Toombs's Brigade
Brigadier General Robert Toombs
Colonel Henry L. Benning
2nd Georgia
15th Georgia
17th Georgia
20th Georgia

Drayton's Brigade
Brigadier General Thomas F. Drayton
50th Georgia
51st Georgia
15th South Carolina

Pickett's Brigade
Brigadier General Richard B. Garnett
8th Virginia
18th Virginia
19th Virginia
28th Virginia
56th Virginia

Kemper's Brigade
Brigadier General J.L. Kemper
1st Virginia
7th Virginia
11th Virginia
17th Virginia
24th Virginia

Jenkins's Brigade
Colonel Joseph Walker
1st South Carolina (Volunteers)
2nd South Carolina Rifles
5th South Carolina
6th South Carolina
4th South Carolina Battalion
Palmetto (South Carolina) Sharpshooters

<u>Anderson's Brigade</u>
Colonel George T. Anderson
1st Georgia (Regulars)
7th Georgia
8th Georgia
9th Georgia
11th Georgia

<u>Artillery</u>
Fauquier (Virginia) Artillery (Stribling's Battery)
Loudoun (Virginia) Artillery (Rogers's Battery)
Turner (Virginia) Artillery (Leake's Battery)
Wise (Virginia) Artillery (J.. Brown's Battery)

WALKER'S DIVISION
Brigadier General John Walker

<u>Walker's Brigade</u>
Colonel Vannoy H. Manning
3rd Arkansas
27th North Carolina
46th North Carolina
48th North Carolina
30th Virginia
French's (Virginia) Battery

<u>Ransom's Brigade</u>
Brigadier General Robert Ransom Jr.
24th North Carolina
25th North Carolina
35th North Carolina
49th North Carolina
Branch's Field Artillery (Virginia)

HOOD'S DIVISION
Brigadier General John Bell Hood

<u>Hood's Brigade</u>
Colonel William T. Wofford

18th Georgia
Hampton (South Carolina) Legion
1st Texas
4th Texas
5th Texas

Law's Brigade
Colonel Evander M. Law
4th Alabama
2nd Mississippi
11th Mississippi
6th North Carolina

Artillery
Major B.F. Frobel
German Artillery (South Carolina)
Palmetto Artillery (South Carolina)
Rowan Artillery (North Carolina)

Evan's Brigade
Brigadier General Nathan G. Evans
Colonel Peter F. Stevens
17th South Carolina
18th South Carolina
22nd South Carolina
23rd South Carolina
Holcombe (South Carolina) Legion
Macbeth (South Carolina) Artillery

ARTILLERY

Washington (Louisiana) Artillery
Colonel J.B. Walton
1st Company, Captain C.W. Squires
2nd Company, Captain J.B. Richardson
3rd Company, Captain M.B. Miller
4th Company, Captain B.F. Eshleman

Lee's Battalion
Colonel Stephen D. Lee
Ashland (Virginia) Artillery
Bedford (Virginia) Artillery
Brooks (South Carolina) Artillery
Eubank's (Virginia) Battery
Madison (Louisiana) Light Artillery
Parker's (Virginia) Battery

JACKSON'S COMMAND
Major General Thomas J. Jackson

EWELL'S DIVISION
Brigadier General Alexander Lawton (w)
Brigadier General Jubal Early

Lawton's Brigade
Colonel Marcellus Douglass (k)
Major J.H. Lowe
Colonel John Lamar
13th Georgia
26th Georgia
31st Georgia
38th Georgia
60th Georgia
61st Georgia

Early's Brigade
Brigadier General Jubal Early
Colonel William Smith
13th Virginia
25th Virginia
31st Virginia
44th Virginia
49th Virginia
52nd Virginia
58th Virginia

Trimble's Brigade
Colonel James A. Walker
15th Alabama
12th Georgia
21st Georgia
21st North Carolina
1st North Carolina Battalion

Hays's Brigade
Brigadier General Harry T. Hays
5th Louisiana
6th Louisiana
7th Louisiana
8th Louisiana
14th Louisiana

Artillery
Major A.R. Courtney
Charlottesville (Virginia) Artillery (Carrington's Battery)
Chesapeake (Maryland) Artillery (Brown's Battery)
Courtney (Virginia) Artillery (Latimer's Battery)
Johnson's (Virginia) Battery
Louisiana Guard Artillery (D'Aquin's Battery)
First Maryland Battery (Dement's Battery)
Staunton (Virginia) Artillery (Balthis's Battery)

A.P. HILL'S DIVISION
Major General Ambrose Powell Hill

Branch's Brigade
Brigadier General L. O'Branch (k)
Colonel James H. Lane
7th North Carolina
18th North Carolina
28th North Carolina
33rd North Carolina
37th North Carolina

Gregg's Brigade
Brigadier General Maxcy Gregg
1st South Carolina (Provisional Army)
1st South Carolina Rifles
12th South Carolina
13th South Carolina
14th South Carolina

Field's Brigade
Colonel John Brockenbrough
40th Virginia
47th Virginia
55th Virginia
22nd Virginia Battalion

Archer's Brigade
Brigadier General James J. Archer
5th Alabama Battalion
19th Georgia
1st Tennessee (Provisional Army)
7th Tennessee
14th Tennessee

Pender's Brigade
Brigadier General William D. Pender
16th North Carolina
22nd North Carolina
34th North Carolina
38th North Carolina

Thomas's Brigade
Colonel Edward Thomas
14th Georgia
35th Georgia
45th Georgia
49th Georgia

Forlorn Hopes

<u>Artillery</u>
Lieutenant Colonel Reuben L. Walker
Branch (North Carolina) Artillery (A.C. Latham's Battery)
Crenshaw's (Virginia) Battery
Fredericksburg (Virginia) Artillery (Braxton's Battery)
Letcher (Virginia) Artillery (Davidson's Battery)
Middlesex (Virginia) Artillery (Fleet's Battery)
Pee Dee (South Carolina) Artillery (McIntosh's Battery)
Purcell (Virginia) Artillery (Pegram's Battery)

JACKSON'S DIVISION
Brigadier General John R. Jones (w)
Brigadier General William E. Starke (k)
Colonel A.J. Grigsby

<u>Stonewall Brigade</u>
Colonel A.J. Grigsby
Major H.J. Williams
2nd Virginia
4th Virginia
5th Virginia
27th Virginia
33rd Virginia

<u>Taliaferro's Brigade</u>
Colonel James W. Jackson
47th Alabama
48th Alabama
10th Virginia
23rd Virginia
37th Virginia

<u>J.R. Jones's Brigade</u>
Captain John Penn (w) (c)
Captain A.C. Page
Captain R.W. Withers
21st Virginia
42nd Virginia
48th Virginia
1st Virginia Battalion

Starke's Brigade
Brigadier General William Starke
Colonel Leroy A. Stafford
Colonel E. Pendleton
1st Louisiana
2nd Louisiana
9th Louisiana
10th Louisiana
15th Louisiana
Coppens's (Louisiana) Battalion

Artillery
Major L.M. Shumaker
Alleghany (Virginia) Artillery (Carpenter's Battery)
Brockenbrough's (Maryland) Battery
Danville (Virginia) Artillery (Wooding's Battery)
Hampden (Virginia)Artillery (Caskie's Battery)
Lee (Virginia) Battery (Raine's Battery)
Rockbridge (Virginia) Artillery (Poague's Battery)

D.H. HILL'S DIVISION
Major General Daniel Harvey Hill

Ripley's Brigade
Brigadier General Roswell Ripley (w)
Colonel George Doles
4th Georgia
44th Georgia
1st North Carolina
3rd North Carolina

Rodes's Brigade
Brigadier General Robert E. Rodes
3rd Alabama
5th Alabama
6th Alabama
12th Alabama
26th Alabama

Garland's Brigade
Colonel Duncan McRae
5th North Carolina
12th North Carolina
13th North Carolina
20th North Carolina
23rd North Carolina

G.B. Anderson's Brigade
Brigadier General George B. Anderson (mw)
Colonel Risden T. Bennett
2nd North Carolina
4th North Carolina
14th North Carolina
30th North Carolina

Colquitt's Brigade
Colonel Alfred H. Colquitt
13th Alabama
6th Georgia
23rd Georgia
27th Georgia
28th Georgia

Artillery
Major Pierson
Hardaway's (Alabama) Battery
Jefferson Davis (Alabama) Artillery
Jones's (Virginia) Battery
King William (Virginia) Artillery

RESERVE ARTILLERY
Brigadier General William N. Pendleton

Brown's Battalion
Colonel J. Thompson Brown
Powhatan Artillery (Dance's Battery)
Richmond Howitzers, 2nd Company (Watson's Battery)
Richmond Howitzers, 3rd Company (Smith's Battery)

Salem Artillery (Hupp's Battery)
Williamsburg Artillery (Coke's Battery)

Cutts's Battalion
Lieutenant Colonel A.S. Cutts
Blackshears's (Georgia) Battery
Irwin (Georgia) Artillery (Lane's Battery)
Lloyd's (North Carolina) Battery
Patterson's (Georgia) Battery
Ross's (Georgia) Battery

Jones's Battalion
Major Hilary P. Jones
Morris (Virginia) Artillery R.C.M. Page's Battery)
Orange (Virginia) Artillery (Peyton's Battery)
Turner's (Virginia) Battery
Wimbish's (Virginia) Battery

Nelson's Battalion
Major William Nelson
Amherst (Virginia) Artillery (Kirkpatrick's Battery)
Fluvanna (Virginia) Artillery (Ancell's Battery)
Huckstep's (Virginia) Battery
Johnson's (Virginia) Battery
Milledge (Georgia) Artillery (Milledge's Battery)

Miscellaneous
Cutshaw's (Virginia) Battery
Dixie (Virginia) Artillery (Chapman's Battery)
Magruder (Virginia) Artillery (T.J. Page Jr.'s Battery)
Rice's (Virginia) battery, Captain W.H. Rice
Thomas (Virginia) Artillery (E.J. Anderson's Battery)

CAVALRY
Major General Jeb Stuart

Hampton's Brigade
Brigadier General Wade Hampton
1st North Carolina

2nd South Carolina
10th Virginia
Cobb's (Georgia) Legion
Jefferson Davis Legion

Lee's Brigade
Brigadier General Fitzhugh Lee
1st Virginia
3rd Virginia
4th Virginia
5th Virginia
9th Virginia

Robertson's Brigade
Colonel Thomas T. Munford
2nd Virginia
6th Virginia
7th Virginia
12th Virginia
17th Virginia Battalion

Horse Artillery
Captain John Pelham
Chew's (Virginia) Battery
Hart's (South Carolina) Battery
Pelham's (Virginia) Battery

Notes

Chapter 1

1. Private John W. Stevens's account in Woodhead, *Antietam*, 16.
2. Wiley, *Road to Appomattox*; McPherson, *Crossroads of Freedom*.
3. Wiley, *Road to Appomattox*, 46–49; Long, *Civil War Day by Day*.
4. Wiley, *Road to Appomattox*, 47.
5. Long, *Civil War Day by Day*, 135–36.
6. Wiley, *Road to Appomattox*, 49–50; McPherson, *Crossroads of Freedom*; 28–34.
7. Wiley, *Road to Appomattox*, 50.
8. Long, *Civil War Day by Day*, 104, 173, 189–90.
9. Ibid., 238–43.
10. Cooling, *Counter-Thrust*, 138–227.
11. Frye, "Under Fire," 70–85; Franklin to McClellan Letter, Stahl Collection.
12. Harsh, *Sounding the Shallows*, 182–83.

Chapter 2

13. Rafuse, *McClellan's War*, 10–14, 30–49, 68–82.
14. Harsh, *Sounding the Shallows*, 103; interview with Lance Herdegen, 2006; 5th Maryland file, Antietam National Battlefield (ANB); Rosen, *Jewish Confederates*, 107–08; Simpson, *Hood's Texas Brigade*, 545; Brooks and Jones, *Lee's Foreign Legion*, 79–87; Inscription on Catawba Monument, Fort Mill, SC; Alexander, "Hispanics in the Civil War" and "Antietam Stories of Human Interest," *Blue and Gray*, 19, 48–49.
15. Armstrong, *Unfurl Those Colors*, 29–30, 32, 78.
16. Alexander, "Two Great American Armies."

17. Alexander, *126th Pennsylvania*, 3; D. Scott Hartwig, "Who Would Not Be a Soldier: The Volunteers of 62 in the Maryland Campaign" in Gallagher, *Antietam Campaign*, 143–68.

18. Warner, *Generals in Blue*, 57, 159, 233, 309, 378–79, 489; Luvass and Nelson, *Guide to the Battle of Antietam*, xii.

19. Harsh, *Sounding the Shallows*, 102–06.

20. Davis and Hoffman, *Confederate General*, 102–05, 121–27, 150–51.

21. Harsh, *Sounding the Shallows*, 202.

22. Todd, *American Military Equipage*, vol. 1, 57.

23. U.S. War Department, *War of the Rebellion*, series 1, vol. 19, part II, 487–88 (hereafter cited as *OR*).

24. Angela Kirkem Davis Diary, Antietam National Battlefield.

25. Kimmel, "Confederate Infantryman at Antietam," 8–15; Todd, *American Military Equipage*, vol. 2, 421–28.

26. Kerr, *Civil War Surgeon*, 72.

27. Oeffinger, *A Soldier's General*, 154.

28. Bilby, *Remember Fontenoy*, 147–51.

29. Bilby, *Civil War Firearms*, 26–27.

30. Keith S. Bohannon, "Dirty, Ragged and Ill Provided For: Confederate Logistical Problems in the 1862 Maryland Campaign and Their Solutions," in Gallagher, *Antietam Campaign*, 104.

31. Bilby, *Civil War Firearms*, 24.

32. Chiles, "Artillery Hell," 8–16, 41–58; Luvaas and Nelson, xvii–xix.

33. Bohannon, "Dirty, Ragged and Ill Provided For," 105; Starr, *Union Cavalry in the Civil War*, vol. 1, 312–17; Luvass and Nelson, *Guide to the Battle of Antietam*, xvi, xix, xx.

34. Ibid.

Chapter 3

35. Alexander and Walker, "Mumma Farm," 1–6; Williams, *History of Washington County*, 10–36.

36. Scharf, *History of Western Maryland*; Williams, *History of Washington County*; Trowbridge, *The South*, 50.

37. Williams, *History of Washington County*, 17–18, 19; Smith, *Golden Age*, 11–23, 94.

38. Glatfelter, *Pennsylvania Germans*, iii, 15.

39. Nead, Pennsylvania Germans, 62–63; Stapleton, *Memorials of the Huguenots*, iii, viii, 1–25, 33–37, 133–35.

40. Barron and Barron, *History of Sharpsburg*, 44–49; Warfield, *Newspaper History*, chs. 4 and 5.

41. Barron and Barron, *History of Sharpsburg*, 45; Warfield, *Newspaper History*, ch. 6.

42. Interview with canal historian John Frye, February 2, 2005; Walker and Kirkman, *Antietam Farmsteads*, 42.

43. Alexander and Walker, "Mumma Farm," 26–27.

44. Ibid., 27.

45. Wallace, "Reclaiming Forgotten History," 59–63; Walker and Kirkman, *Antietam Farmsteads*, 19–31.

46. Wallace, "Reclaiming Forgotten History," 33–40; GWWO Inc., Miller Farmstead, 1.

47. Reilly, *Battlefield of Antietam*, 22.

48. Alexander and Walker, "Mumma Farm," 34–36.

49. Walker and Kirkman, *Antietam Farmsteads*, 63–75; GWWO, Roulette, HSR, 36–37.

50. Walker and Kirkman, *Antietam Farmsteads*, 77–85.

51. Ibid.

52. Ibid.

53. Ibid.

CHAPTER 4

54. Carman, *Maryland Campaign*, 201–14.

55. 8th Ohio file, ANB.

56. Carman, *Maryland Campaign*, 201–14.

57. Alexander, "Bloodiest Day," 78.

58. Carman, *Maryland Campaign*, 201–14.

59. Hood, *Advance and Retreat*, 43.

60. Alexander, "Bloodiest Day," 78; Carman, *Maryland Campaign*.

61. *OR*, 955; Carman, *Maryland Campaign*, 215.

62. Ibid.

63. Letter home from unidentified Confederate soldier, 5th Alabama file, ANB.

CHAPTER 5

64. Carman, *Maryland Campaign*, 215–19.

65. Robert E.L. Krick, "Defending Lee's Flank: J.E.B. Stuart, John Pelham, and Confederate Artillery on Nicodemus Heights," in Gallagher, *Antietam Campaign*, 192–222.

66. *OR*, 845–46.

67. Ibid., 218.

68. Warner, *Generals in Blue*, 432–33.

69. Clement Evans, ed. *Confederate Military History*, Vol. 14, *Virginia* (N.p., 1899): 676–78.

70. Carman, *Maryland Campaign*, 219.

71. Warner, *General in Blue*, 212–13.

72. 12th Massachusetts file, ANB; Private Prince Dunton, letter, 11th Pennsylvania file, ANB.

73. Taylor, *Glory Was Not Their Companion*, 79–86, 127–28.

74. Davis and Hoffman, *Confederate General*, vol. 3, 78–81.

75. Alexander, *North and South*, 79–80.

76. Ibid.

77. Ibid.

78. Ibid.

79. Jerry Holsworth, "Hood's Texas Brigade in the Maryland Campaign," *Blue and Gray Magazine*, (Summer 1996): 13–20.

80. Ibid.

81. Alexander, *North and South*, 80–81; Carman, *Maryland Campaign*, ch. 16; Luvass and Nelson, *Guide to the Battle of Antietam*, xii; Hartwig in Gallagher, *Antietam Campaign*, 164.

82. Carman, *Maryland Campaign*, 242–50.

83. Ibid.

84. Ibid.

85. Ibid.

CHAPTER 6

86. Stinson, "Operations of Sedgwick's Division," passim.

87. Warner, *Generals in Blue*, 489–90.

88. Ibid.

89. Ibid., 489–90.

90. Stinson, "Operations of Sedgwick's Division."

91. Ibid.

92. Carman, *Maryland Campaign*, 253–76.

93. Jensen, *32nd Virginia Infantry*, 89.

94. 125th Pennsylvania file, ANB.

95. Ibid.

96. Ibid.

97. 15th Massachusetts file, ANB.

98. Soldier's letter to sister, Carrie From Merril, 1st Minnesota file, ANB.

99. Stinson, "Operations of Sedgwick's Division."

100. Armstrong, *Unfurl Those Colors*, 165–205.
101. Stinson, "Analytical Study."
102. Sergeant William H.H. Fithian journal (copy), 28th Pennsylvania file, ANB; Jacob Orth, Medal of Honor File, ANB.
103. 48th Virginia file, ANB.
104. Stinson, "Analytical Study."

Chapter 7

105. Alexander, *North and South*, 85–86.
106. Ibid.
107. Harsh, *Taken at the Flood*, 395–97.
108. Ibid.
109. Ibid.; Carman, *Maryland Campaign*, 277–98.
110. Dwight Stinson, "Federal Penetration of Sunken Road," ANB, 1971.

Chapter 8

111. Carman, *Maryland Campaign*, 329–63.
112. Harsh, *Taken at the Flood*, 400–23.
113. Carman, *Maryland Campaign*, 329–63.
114. Ibid.
115. Ibid.
116. Jacob Bauer Letter, 16th Connecticut file, ANB.
117. Carman, *Maryland Campaign*, 357–62.
118. Ibid.

Chapter 9

119. Nesbitt, Diary, 193–95.
120. Strother, "Personal Recollections," 285–87.
121. Private Edward M. Burrus, letter, copy, 21st Mississippi Infantry file, ANB (original in John C. Burrus Papers, Hill Memorial Library, Louisiana State University).
122. Letter from unidentified soldier of the 145th Pennsylvania Infantry to *Erie Gazette*, October 16, 1862, 145th Pennsylvania Infantry Regimental file, ANB.
123. "Stories Supplied by Hilda Mose." ANB
124. Been letter in Skidmore, *Alford Brothers*, 321–22.
125. "Recollections of John P. Smith: The Battle of Antietam, The History of Antietam and the Hospitals of Antietam, 1895," Smith file, ANB;

Schildt, *Sharpsburg Echo*, 4; "Samuel J. Fletcher: A Short Account of My Army Life," 15th Massachusetts Infantry file, ANB.

126. Stotelmyer, *Bivouacs of the Dead*, 6.

127. Ibid., 12–13; Reilly, *Battlefield of Antietam*, 23.

128. Nelson, *As Grain Falls*, 5–9.

129. Alexander, "Sharpsburg Civilians," 165.

130. Schildt, *Antietam Hospitals*, 27.

131. Smith, "History of Antietam," ANB.

132. "Rebels in the Hospital at Sharpsburg," *Hagerstown Herald and Torchlight*, November 5, 1862, in 16th Mississippi file, ANB.

133. 6th Alabama file, ANB.

134. Davis, "War Reminiscences."

135. James F. Linn Harbaugh, *Mercersburg in War Times*, 2002, 26.

136. Reilly, *Battlefield of Antietam*, 28.

137. Ibid., 20.

138. *Hagerstown Herald and Torchlight.*

139. Luvass and Nelson, *Guide to the Battle of Antietam*, 270–71.

140. Alexander, *North and South*, 11–12.

141. Magner, *Traveller and Company*, 47–48.

142. Steiner, *Disease in the Civil War*, 14–25.

143. Ibid.

144. Jacob Miller letter, December 7, 1862, ANB.

145. Ibid.

146. Michael letter, November 27, 1862, ANB.

147. Roulette HSR, 48.

148. Smith, 118th Pennsylvania, 52.

149. Antietam relic lists, photo lists, bibliographies and human interest stories, ANB.

150. Reilly, *Battlefield of Antietam*, 28.

151. Piper Farm federal court claims, copy, ANB.

152. Wilshin, "Mumma Farm," 7–8, 37–58.

153. Bud Shackleford interview, January 24, 1934, in interviews with local people file, ANB.

154. Carman, *Maryland Campaign*, 469–81; John Nelson in his seminal study, *As Grain Falls Before the Reaper*, has found 12,651 Union casualties for the campaign. This includes killed, wounded, missing, captured or deserted. He states that there were more than 16,000 Union casualties if you include the sick in the area hospitals.

155. Schildt, *Antietam Hospitals*, 2–9, 48.

CHAPTER 10

156. Carman, *Maryland Campaign*, 365.

157. Ibid., 368; McGrath, *Shepherdstown*, 28; Alexander, "Shepherdstown," 1.

158. Carman, *Maryland Campaign*, 371–78; Alexander, "Shepherdstown," 2 ; McGrath, *Shepherdstown*, 32–37.

159. Carman, *Maryland Campaign*, 373–78.

160. Ibid.

161. Ibid.

162. Ibid.

163. Ibid.

164. Harsh, *Sounding the Shallows*, 212–13, 220–21, *OR*, 19; pt. 2, 621, 639, 713.

165. Schildt, *Four Days in October, passim.*

166. Alexander, *126ᵗʰ Pennsylvania*, 117.

167. Alexander, "Antietam Stories," 60–62.

168. Alexander, *126ᵗʰ Pennsylvania*, 122–23.

169. Long, *Civil War Day by Day*, 274–76.

170. Guelzo, *Lincoln's Emancipation Proclamation*, 212–13; Medford, *Emancipation Proclamation*, 22; McPherson, *Crossroads of Freedom*, 141.

CHAPTER 11

171. Montgomery Diary, 43, USAMHI; Smith, *Golden Age*, 96.

172. Stotelmyer, *Bivouacs of the Dead*, 19–27.

173. Ibid.; Beebe, "Finding Antietam,"128–35.

174. Trail, "Remembering Antietam," 154–60.

175. Smith, *Golden Age of Battlefield Preservation*, 5–48.

176. Ibid., 87–113.

177. Ibid.

178. Maryland monument file, ANB.

179. Trail, "Remembering Antietam," 153–68.

180. Cross, *New York at Antietam.*

181. Reilly, *Battlefield of Antietam.*

182. Trail, "Remembering Antietam," 303–06.

183. Cross, *New York at Antietam.*

184. Trail, "Remembering Antietam," 310; Cross, *New York at Antietam.*

185. Smith, *Golden Age of Battlefield Preservation*, 322–24.

186. Snell and Brown, "Antietam National Battlefield," 146–210.

187. Ibid.

188. Ibid.

189. Ibid.

190. Ibid.

191. Sellers, *Preserving Nature*, 182–84.

192. Ibid.

193. Ibid.

194. Alexander and Walker, "Mumma Farm," 86–92.

195. Snell and Brown, "Antietam National Battlefield," 344, 347, 348, 351–55, 359.

196. Alexander, "Antietam Stories," 54–56.

197. Alexander and Walker, "Mumma Farm," 97–98.

198. Patrick Roy file, ANB.

APPENDIX

199. The Volunteer Engineer Brigade, AOP, was on detached duty in Washington during the Maryland Campaign.

200. On detached duty in Washington during the Maryland Campaign.

201. The 16th Maine Infantry joined the 3rd Brigade, 2nd Division, First Corps, on September 9, 1862, but was on detached duty guarding railroad lines since September 13 and was thus not present at the Battle of Antietam.

202. This battery was on detached duty in Washington during the Maryland Campaign.

203. The 1st Division of the Fourth Corps was attached to the Sixth Corps during the Maryland Campaign of 1862. On September 26, 1862, this division was redesignated the 3rd Division, Sixth Corps.

204. General Burnside was in command of the left wing, Army of the Potomac, consisting of the First and Ninth Corps. Brigadier General Jacob Cox was in immediate command of the Ninth Corps.

205. This regiment was on detached duty in Frederick, Maryland, and was not present at the Battle of Antietam.

206. This regiment was on detached duty and was thus not present at Antietam.

207. Ibid.

208. This regiment was on detached duty at Frederick, Maryland, and was thus not present at Antietam.

Bibliography

Primary Sources

Antietam Battlefield Memorial Commission. *Pennsylvania at Antietam*. Harrisburg, PA: Harrisburg Publishing Company, 1906.

Carman, Ezra. *The Maryland Campaign of 1862*. Edited by Joseph Pierro. New York: Routledge, 2008.

Cross, Fred. Scrapbook. 1921. Doug Bast Collection.

Franklin, General William, to General George B. McClellan, September 14, 1862, Letter. Joseph Stahl Collection.

Hood, John Bell. *Advance and Retreat: Personal Experiences in the United States and Confederate States Armies*. Edited by Richard N. Current. Bloomington: Indiana University Press, 1959.

Johnson, Clifton. *Battleground Adventures: The Stories of Dwellers on the Scenes of Conflict in Some of the Most Notable Battles of the Civil War*. Boston: Houghton Mifflin Company, 1915.

Montgomery, James. Diary. June 28, 1864. USAMHI. Civil War Miscellany Collection.

Nesbitt, Otho. *Windmills of Time*. Diary edited by David Wiles. Clear Spring, MD, 1981.

Nye, Captain George, 10th Maine, letter to wife. Nicholas Picerno Collection.

Oeffinger, John C., ed. *A Soldier's General: The Civil War Letters of Major General Lafayette McLaws*. Chapel Hill: University of North Carolina Press, 2002.

Regimental Committee. *History of the One Hundred and Twenty-fifth Regiment Pennsylvania Volunteers, 1862–1863*. Philadelphia: J.P. Lippincott, 1907.

Reilly, O.T. *The Battlefield of Antietam*. Hagerstown, PA, 1906.

Skidmore, Richard, ed. *The Alford Brothers: "We All Must Dye Sooner or Later."* Hanover, IN, 1995.

Strother, David Hunter. "Personal Recollections of the War by a Virginian." *Harpers New Monthly Magazine*, February 1868.

Trowbridge, John Townsend. *The South: A Tour of Its Battlefields and Ruined Cities, A Journey through the Desolated States, and Talks with the People, 1867.* Macon, GA: Mercer University Press, 2006.

U.S. War Department. *The War of the Rebellion: A Compilation of the Official Records of the Union and Confederate Armies.* 128 vols. Washington, D.C.: Government Printing Office, 1880–1901.

Woodhead, Henry, ed. *Antietam: Voices of the Civil War.* N.p.: Time Life Books, 1996.

SECONDARY SOURCES

Alexander, Ted, ed. *The 126th Pennsylvania.* Shippensburg, PA: Beidel Printing House, Inc., 1984.

Allabach, Sara. *Mission 66 Visitor Centers: The History of a Building Type.* Washington, D.C.: U.S. Department of the Interior, 2000.

Armstrong, Marion V., Jr. *Unfurl Those Colors: McClellan, Sumner, and the Second Army Corps in the Antietam Campaign.* Tuscaloosa: University of Alabama Press, 2008.

Barron, Lee, and Barbara Barron. *The History of Sharpsburg.* Sharpsburg, MD, 1972.

Bates, Samuel P. *History of Pennsylvania Volunteers, 1861–65.* 5 vols. Harrisburg, PA: B. Singerly, 1871.

———. *Martial Deeds of Pennsylvania.* Philadelphia: T.H. Davis and Co., 1876.

Bilby, Joseph G. *Civil War Firearms: Their Historical Background, Tactical Use and Modern Collecting and Shooting.* Conshocken, PA: Combined Books, Inc., 1996.

———. *Remember Fontenoy: The 69th New York and the Irish Brigade in the Civil War.* Highstown, NJ: Longstreet House, 1995.

Brooks, Thomas Walter, and Michael Dan Jones. *Lee's Foreign Legion: A History of the 10th Louisiana.* Gravenhurst, ON: Watts Printing, 1995.

Coker, Michael D. *The Battle of Port Royal.* Charleston, SC: The History Press, 2009.

Cooling, Benjamin Franklin. *Counter-Thrust: From the Peninsula to the Antietam.* Lincoln: University of Nebraska Press, 2007.

Davis, William C., and Julie Hoffman, eds. *The Confederate General.* N.p.: National Historical Society, 1991.

Drake, Julia Angeline, and James Ridgely Orndorff. *From Mill Wheel to Plowshare: The Story of the Christian Orndorff Family to the Social and Industrial History of the United States.* Cedar Rapids, IA, 1938.

Eberly, Robert E., Jr. *Bouquets from the Cannon's Mouth: Soldiering with the Eighth Regiment of the Pennsylvania Reserves.* Shippensburg, PA: White Mane Books, 2005.

Ernst, Kathleen A. *Too Afraid to Cry: Maryland Civilians in the Antietam Campaign.* Mechanicsburg, PA: Stackpole Books, 1999.

Fishel, Edwin C. *The Secret War for the Union: Intelligence in the Civil War.* Boston: Houghton Mifflin Company, 1996.

Frassanito, William A. *Antietam: The Photographic Legacy of America's Bloodiest Day.* New York, 1978.

Frye, Dennis. *Antietam Revealed.* Collingswood, NJ: C.W. Historicals, LLC, 2004.

Gallagher, Gary, ed. *Antietam: Essays on the 1862 Maryland Campaign.* Kent, OH: The Kent State University Press, 1989.————. *The Antietam Campaign.* Chapel Hill: University of North Carolina Press, 1999.

Gibbs, Joseph. *Three Years in the Bloody Eleventh: The Campaigns of a Pennsylvania Reserves Regiment.* University Park: The Pennsylvania State University Press, n.d.

Glatfelter, Charles H. *The Pennsylvania Germans: A Brief Account of Their Influence on Pennsylvania.* University Park, PA, 1990.

Goff, Richard D. *Confederate Supply.* Durham, NC: Duke University Press, 1969.

Guelzo, Allen G. *Lincoln's Emancipation Proclamation: The End of Slavery in America.* New York: Simon and Schuster, 2004.

Harsh, Joseph L. *Sounding the Shallows: A Confederate Companion for the Maryland Campaign.* Kent, OH: Kent State University Press, 2000.

————. *Taken at the Flood: Robert E. Lee and Confederate Strategy in the Maryland Campaign of 1862.* Kent, OH: Kent State University Press, 1999

Holzer, Harold, Edna Greene Medford and Frank J. Williams. *The Emancipation Proclamation: Three Views.* Baton Rouge: Louisiana State University Press, 2006.

Hays, Helen Ashe. *The Antietam and its Bridges.* New York: G.P. Putnam's Sons, 1910.

Herdegen, Lance J. *The Men Stood Like Iron: How the Iron Brigade Won Its Name.* Bloomington, IN: University Press, 1997.

Hewitt, Lawrence Lee, and Arthur W. Bergeron Jr., ed. *Louisianans in the Civil War.* Columbia: University of Missouri Press, 2002.

Holzer, Howard, Edna Greene Medford and Frank J. Williams. *The Emancipation Proclamation: Three Views.* Baton Rouge: Louisiana State University Press, 2006.

Jensen, Les. *32nd Virginia Infantry.* Lynchburg, VA: H.E. Howard, Inc., 1990.

Johnson, Curt, and Richard C. Anderson Jr. *Artillery Hell: The Employment of Artillery at Antietam.* College Station: Texas A&M University Press, 1995.

Jones, Terry L. *Lee's Tigers: The Louisiana Infantry in the Army of Northern Virginia.* Baton Rouge: Louisiana State University Press, 1987.

Kerr, Paul B. *Civil War Surgeon: Biography of James Langstaff Dunn, MD*. N.p.: AuthorHouse, 2005.

Long, E.B., with Barbara Long. *The Civil War Day by Day: An Almanac 1861–1865*. New York: Da Capo Press, Inc., 1971.

Lonn, Ella. *Foreigners in the Confederacy*. Chapel Hill: University of North Carolina Press, 1940.

———. *Foreigners in the Union Army and Navy*. Baton Rouge: Louisiana State University Press, 1940.

Luvass, Jay, and Harold W. Nelson. *Guide to the Battle of Antietam: The Maryland Campaign of 1862*. Lawrence: University Press of Kansas, 1987.

Magner, Blake. *Traveller and Company: The Horses of Gettysburg*. Gettysburg, PA: Farnsworth House, 1995.

McGrath, Thomas A. *Shepherdstown: Last Clash of the Antietam Campaign, September 19–20, 1862*. Lynchburg, VA: Schroeder Publications, 2008.

McPherson, James M. *Crossroads of Freedom: Antietam, The Battle That Changed the Course of the Civil War*. New York: Oxford University Press, 2002.

Murfin, James V. *The Gleam of Bayonets: The Battle of Antietam and Robert E. Lee's Maryland Campaign, September 1862*. Baton Rouge: Louisiana State University Press, 1965.

Nead, Daniel W. *The Pennsylvania Germans in the Settlement of Western Maryland*. N.p., n.d.

Nelson, John H. *As Grain Falls Before the Reaper: The Federal Hospital Sites and Identified Federal Casualties at Antietam*. CD. Hagerstown, MD, n.d.

Poffenberger, Thomas. *From Germany to Antietam: The Early History of the Pfaffenberger Family*. N.p.: Xlibris Corporation, 2003.

Rafuse, Ethan S. *McClellan's War: The Failure of Moderation in the Struggle for the Union*. Bloomington: Indiana University Press, 2005.

Reaman, G. Elmore. *The Trail of the Huguenots in Europe, the United States, South Africa and Canada*. Baltimore, 1966.

Rosen, Robert N. *The Jewish Confederates*. Columbia: University of South Carolina Press, 2000.

Scharf, J. Thomas. *History of Western Maryland*. 2 vols. Philadelphia, 1882.

Schildt, John W. *Antietam Hospitals*. Chewsville, MD: Antietam Publications, 1987.

———. *Drums Along the Antietam*. Chewsville, MD: Antietam Publications, 1972.

———. *The Sharpsburg Echo*. Hagerstown, MD, 1970.

Sears, Stephen W. *Landscape Turned Red: The Battle of Antietam*. New York, Houghton Mifflin Company, 1983.

Sellers, Ricahard West. *Preserving Nature in the National Parks: A History*. New Haven, CT: Yale University Press, 1997.

Simpson, Harold B. *Hood's Texas Brigade: A Compendium*. Hillsboro, TX: Hill Junior College Press, 1977.

———. *Hood's Texas Brigade: Lee's Grenadier Guard.* Waco, TX, 1970.

Smith, Timothy B. *The Golden Age of Battlefield Preservation: The Decade of the 1890s and the Establishment of America's First Five Military Parks.* Knoxville: University of Tennessee, 2008.

Stapleton, Reverend A. *Memorials of the Huguenots in America; With Special Reference to Their Emigration to Pennsylvania.* Carlisle, PA, 1901.

Starr, Stephen Z. *The Union Cavalry in the Civil War.* Vol. 1. Baton Rouge: Louisiana State University Press, 1979.

Steiner, Paul E. *Disease in the Civil War: Natural Biological Warfare in 1861–1865.* Springfield, MA, 1968.

Stotelmyer, Steven R. *The Bivouacs of the Dead: The Story of Those Who Died at Antietam and South Mountain.* Linthicum, MD: Toomey Press, 1992.

Taylor, Paul. *Glory Was Not Their Companion: The Twenty-sixth New York Volunteer Infantry in the Civil War.* Jefferson, NC: McFarland and Company, Inc., 2005.

Todd, Frederick P. *American Military Equipage: 1851–1872.* Vols. 1 and 2. Providence, RI: Company of Military Historians, 1977.

Trout, Robert J. *Galloping Thunder: The Stuart Horse Artillery Battalion.* Mechanicsburg, PA: Stackpole Books, 2002.

Ural, Susannah Bruce. *The Harp and the Eagle: Irish-American Volunteers and the Union Army, 1861–1865.* New York: New York University Press, 2006.

Walker, Keven, and K.C. Kirkman. *Antietam Farmsteads: A Guide to the Battlefield Landscape.* Sharpsburg: Western Maryland Interpretive Association, 2010.

Warner, Ezra J. *Generals in Blue: Lives of the Union Commanders.* Baton Rouge: Louisiana State University Press, 1964.

Wiley, Bell Irvin. *The Road to Appomattox.* Baton Rouge: Louisiana State University Press, 1956.

Williams, Thomas J.C. *A History of Washington County Maryland.* Hagerstown, MD, 1906.

Wyckoff, Mac. *A History of the 3rd South Carolina Infantry: 1861–65.* Fredericksburg, VA: Sergeant Kirkland's Museum and Historical Society, Inc., 1995.

ARTICLES

Alexander, Ted. "Antietam Stories of Human Interest and Sites Off the Beaten Path." *Blue and Gray Magazine*, 5.20, no. 1 (Fall 2002).

———. "Antietam: The Bloodiest Day." *North and South Magazine* 5, no. 7 (October 2002): 76–89.

———. "Antietam: Two Great American Armies Engage in Combat." *Civil War Times* (August 2006).

————. "Destruction, Disease, and Death: The Battle of Antietam and the Sharpsburg Civilians." *The Maryland Campaign and Its Aftermath: Civil War Regiment* 6, no. 2 (n.d.): 143–73.

————. "Forgotten Valor: Off the Beaten Path at Antietam." *Blue and Gray Magazine* 13 (1995).

Chiles, Paul. "Artillery Hell: The Guns of Antietam." *Blue and Gray Magazine* (n.d.).

Kimmel, Ross M. "The Confederate Infantryman at Antietam, 1862." *Military Illustrated* 17 (February/March 1989): 8–15.

UNPUBLISHED WORKS

Alexander, Ted, and Keven Walker. "Mumma Farm Cultural Landscape Report." Draft. Antietam National Battlefield.

Armstrong, Marian V. "Opposing the Second Corps at Antietam." Unpublished ms., 2010.

Beebe, Wilson H., Jr. "Finding Antietam: Essays on the Memory and Meaning of Place." Red Bank, NJ, 2008.

Frye, Dennis. "Under Fire: Harpers Ferry in the Civil War." Harpers Ferry NHP.

GWWO, Inc. "Newcomer Barn." Historic Structure Report, May 20, 2004.

————. "Roulette House." Historic Structure Report, March 2006.

Snell, Charles W., and Sharon A. Brown. "Antietam National Battlefield and National Cemetery, Sharpsburg, Maryland: An Administrative History." Washington, D.C.: U.S. Department of the Interior/ National Park Service, 1986.

Snyder, Timothy R. "Trembling in the Balance: The Chesapeake and Ohio Canal During the Civil War." Unpublished ms., 2010.

Stinson, Dwight E., Jr. "Analytical Study of Action of Greene's Division." Antietam National Battlefield Site, February 2, 1961.

————. "Federal Penetration of Sunken Road." Antietam National Battlefield Site, 1971.

————. "Operations of Sedgwick's Division in the West Woods." Antietam National Battlefield Site, March 1962.

"Stories Supplied by Hilda Mose." In the collection of Pat Holland, Sharpsburg, MD.

Tepper, Audrey T. "The Mumma Barn." Historic Structure Report, April 2000.

Trail, Susan W. "Remembering Antietam: Commemoration and Preservation of a Civil War Battlefield." PhD diss., University of Maryland, College Park, 2005.

Wallace, Edith B. "Reclaiming Forgotten History: Preserving Rural African-American Cultural Resources in Washington County, Maryland." Master's thesis, Goucher College, 2003.

Wilshin, Francis. "Mumma Farm, Piper Farm and Sherrick Farm." Historic Structure Report, August 28, 1969.

HISTORIC STRUCTURE REPORTS (HSR) ANTIETAM NATIONAL BATTLEFIELD

Miller Farm
Mumma Farm
Piper Farm
Roulette Farm

ANTIETAM NATIONAL BATTLEFIELD REGIMENTAL FILES

3rd Pennsylvania Cavalry
8th Ohio Infantry
11th Connecticut Infantry
15th Massachusetts Infantry
16th Connecticut Infantry
16th Mississippi
21st Mississippi Infantry
30th Virginia Infantry
125th Pennsylvania Infantry
145th Pennsylvania Infantry

Index

About the Author

Ted Alexander is the chief historian at the Antietam National Battlefield, where he has worked for more than twenty-six years. He is the author, editor or contributor to ten books on the Civil War and other aspects of American history. Ted is also the author of more than two hundred articles and book reviews for publications such as the *Civil War Times, Blue and Gray, North and South* and the *Washington Times*.

Ted has a BA in history from the University of Maryland, College Park, and an MA in history from the University of Maryland, Baltimore County.

Ted is a U.S. Marine Corps veteran of Vietnam, where he served a tour and a half and was awarded the Navy Commendation Medal with Combat V.

He is the founder and coordinator of the very popular Chambersburg Civil War Seminars. Through these events, Ted has been instrumental in helping to raise more than $150,000 for battlefield preservation.

Currently, he is serving as a consultant for the upcoming HBO miniseries *To Appomattox*.

Visit us at
www.historypress.net